W0246606

SHAPING

THE

FUTURE

OF

WORK

ADVANCE PRAISE FOR THE BOOK

'Dr Chandra's extensive experience as a business leader in the HR domain, combined with his research and academic background, shines through in every chapter. The book offers a fresh perspective on the *future of work*, expertly balancing business challenges, social context and the behavioural aspects of human dynamics. Enterprise leaders will leverage this book to navigate topline, bottom line and every line of business'—Pankaj Bansal, founder, PeopleStrong and Taggd; co-founder, Caret Capital; and board member, Karmayogi Bharat

'Chandra has written a timely and interesting book on how trends in the *future of work* might help India foster spatial inclusion of talent and the consequences of not doing so. The book is well researched and contextualizes both the opportunities and challenges of the phenomenon to the Indian context'—Prithwiraj Choudhury, Lumry Family Associate Professor of Business Administration, Harvard Business School, and included in the 2023 Forbes Future of Work-50 list

'Chandra Sripada has built on the existing research around remote and other flexible work arrangements to make a compelling case for how these can be leveraged to generate inclusive employment in India. Policymakers, industry bodies, CEOs and HR leaders will find this book thought provoking and stimulating. The book presents an interesting and unique thesis on the *future of work*. It inspires us to think of the need to shape the *future of work* to be an inclusive one and forces us to confront key challenges such as decent jobs for rural talent, bridging the rural–urban gap, preventing painful migration, decongesting cities and building inclusive economies'—Ravi S. Gajendran, professor and department chair, Global Leadership and Management (GLAM), College of Business, Florida International University

'The forces that shape the *future of work* play out across the world. Yet, to truly understand them we need to focus. In this marvellous book, Chandra does just that for India, persuasively and thoroughly describing the technological, demographic and social trends that will shape work in India. And, more importantly, he has an impassioned vision of how work in India could serve society and support the individual worker. A crucial book for anyone who wants to understand the *future of work* and who cares about how work will evolve in India'—Lynda Gratton, professor of management practice in organizational behaviour, London Business School, and globally acclaimed *future of work* thought leader

'Chandrasekhar Sripada's book *Shaping the Future of Work* offers a comprehensive and insightful exploration of the evolving work landscape, particularly in the context of the Covid-19 pandemic and beyond. Covering a range of topics from the rise of remote and flexible work arrangements to the critical inclusion of human capital, Sripada delves into how Gen Z will shape the flexibility agenda and how organizations can build future-ready models. This book is a must-read for anyone looking to understand and navigate the dynamic shifts in work culture and organizational strategies in India and globally'—Amitabh Kant, India's G20 Sherpa, former CEO, NITI Aayog, and author of the award-winning book *Made in India*

'This is a definitive book on the *future of work* and how the businesses, CEOs and policymakers must shape it for India. The book makes a persuasive case for fostering flexible work models like remote work and gig work and leveraging them to unleash the vast human capital of India, especially in our tier-3 and tier-4 towns. A must-read for all those interested in knowing how flexibility can be a game changer not only for firms but also for the nation—in creating more inclusive employment'—Rohit Kapoor, CEO, Food Marketplace, Swiggy

'Driven by the experience of Covid-19 and the rapid diffusion of new transformational technologies like AI and ML, discussions on the *future of work* dominate contemporary policy and management discourse. In this distinctive book, Chandra Sripada casts aside technological determinism to take a people-centric view of how India can craft its own *future of work* for the benefit of its 1.4 billion people. This is an important and original contribution to the field'—Rishikesha T. Krishnan, professor of strategy, Ram Charan Chair professor in Innovation and Leadership and director, Indian Institute of Management Bangalore

'India is poised to be the office of the world, contributing to over 24.3 per cent of the incremental global workforce over the next decade. In this timely and insightful book, the author puts forth his views on the *future of work* model specific to India that will help bridge the urban–rural divide in employment and help us capitalize on the demographic dividend. Based on the learnings from the post-Covid-era work model, the book argues for more remote working opportunities and inclusive flexibility options that will enable the youth from tier-3 and tier-4 cities to join the organized workforce, across multiple industries'—Rajesh Nambiar, chairman and managing director, Cognizant India, and chairperson, Nasscom

'The book offers practical strategies for organizations to navigate the *future of work*, making it a valuable resource for business leaders and HR professionals. It combines current trends with forward-looking predictions, providing a well-rounded perspective of the future workplace. The actionable insights and real-world examples make the book an engaging and informative read. Overall, *Shaping the Future of Work* by Chandrasekhar

Sripada is a thought-provoking and insightful guide that prepares readers for the inevitable changes in the workplace, emphasizing the need for adaptability, continuous learning and a human-centric approach'—Alok Ohrie, president and managing director, Dell Technologies India

'Chandra's proposition is an interesting combination of idealism and practicality. It supports the Gandhian dream implemented through modern technology (communication and computing) while recognizing the Herculean task of policy reform as well as the behaviour change necessary to realize the dream. A very compulsive read'—R.S. Pawar, chairman and co-founder, NIIT Limited, and founder, NIIT University

'Chandra's writing is both crisp and engaging, offering a hopeful blueprint for harnessing new technologies to drive inclusive job growth in India. Policymakers aiming to broaden employment opportunities and business leaders seeking to diversify their organizations will discover valuable, testable hypotheses within these pages'—Madan Pillutla, dean and professor of organizational behaviour, Indian School of Business

'Is your job future-proof? The world of work is undergoing a seismic shift. Automation, AI and the gig economy are transforming industries at an unprecedented pace. *Shaping the Future of Work* equips you to navigate this dynamic landscape. This insightful guide explores the key trends shaping the workplace, from the rise of remote work to the demand for new skill sets. Learn how to identify in-demand jobs, develop essential skills such as adaptability and critical thinking, and build a career that thrives in the face of change'—Jayesh Ranjan, special chief secretary for Information Technology, Electronics and Communications (ITE&C), and industries and commerce departments, Government of Telangana

'The theme of the book and its contents are very timely and will illuminate many minds with the need for flexibility and innovative thinking in our approach to work. I am sure the book will help all categories of people— policymakers, leaders from various sectors, owners, entrepreneurs, managers, teachers, students, CEOs, CXOs, CHROs and planners at the national level, as well as all states and sectors—understand ways to take work to people, prevent migration, create happiness at work and develop and deploy the massive potential of human capital in our country and enable Bharat and India to maximize the demographic dividend we have been talking about all these years. It is very well written and easy to read, with compelling and convincing arguments, illustrations, examples and even research support to change and firm up our attitudes towards change and flexibility at work. This sets a clear direction for all those interested in defining and determining the future course of work. This book busts the myth that remote work is only for the IT sector and white-collar jobs with examples from a number of sectors including FMCG, pharma, infrastructure, sales, quality and lab testing, etc. The discourse on the *future of work* is largely led by Western narratives and this book is very contemporary and very Indian at the same time'—T.V. Rao, chairman, T.V. Rao Learning Systems, former professor at IIM Ahmedabad and well-known Human Resource Development guru

'Dr Chandrasekhar Sripada, well-respected HR practitioner and academic has brought years of his thought leadership to bear on this timely and extremely relevant book on the *future of work*. He makes a brilliant case for how flexible HR and people practices can be game changing for the nation. All HR professionals, CEOs, business leaders and policymakers must read this book to gain a wider perspective of the immense possibilities the *future of work* presents, especially for the ascending India. This is even more important from the Vision 2047 standpoint, by which time India aspires to gain the developed country status'—Prem Singh, president, Group HR, J.K. Organization, and national president, National HRD Network

'In the book *Shaping the Future of Work*, Chandra draws from his experience of several years of corporate leadership and his academic research covering the After Covid (AC) paradigm changes in the tenets of work: type, place, nature, expectations from the "employer" and "employee". Chandra further delves into how the workforce demographics and the technological advancement have significantly changed the fundamental ideas about the definition of work, workplace, manager and leadership styles, and organization design. Interestingly, the discussion goes beyond the classical white-collar roles and also covers various scenarios related to the shop floor. Thought provoking and a must-read for any manager or a leader looking to shape their strategy about talent and unleash the human capital for the twenty-first century'—Ashwin Yardi, CEO, Capgemini Technology Services India, and member, Group Executive Committee

SHAPING
THE
FUTURE
OF
WORK

**Building Flexible Work Options and
Unleashing the Human Capital of *Bhārat***

CHANDRASEKHAR SRIPADA

PENGUIN
BUSINESS

An imprint of Penguin Random House

PENGUIN BUSINESS

Penguin Business is an imprint of the Penguin Random House group of companies
whose addresses can be found at global.penguinrandomhouse.com

Published by Penguin Random House India Pvt. Ltd
4th Floor, Capital Tower 1, MG Road,
Gurugram 122 002, Haryana, India

Penguin
Random House
India

First published in Penguin Business by Penguin Random House India 2024

Copyright © Chandrasekhar Sripada 2024

All rights reserved

10 9 8 7 6 5 4 3 2

The views and opinions expressed in this book are the author's own and the
facts are as reported by him which have been verified to the extent possible,
and the publishers are not in any way liable for the same.

Please note that no part of this book may be used or reproduced in any manner
for the purpose of training artificial intelligence technologies or systems.

ISBN 9780143469032

Typeset in Sabon LT Std by Manipal Technologies Limited, Manipal
Printed at Replika Press Pvt. Ltd, India

This book is sold subject to the condition that it shall not, by way of trade
or otherwise, be lent, resold, hired out, or otherwise circulated without the
publisher's prior consent in any form of binding or cover other than that in
which it is published and without a similar condition including this condition
being imposed on the subsequent purchaser.

www.penguin.co.in

MIX
Paper | Supporting
responsible forestry
FSC™ C016779

Contents

Introduction

The all-pervading disease of the modern world is the total imbalance between city and countryside, an imbalance in terms of wealth, power, culture, attraction and hope. The former has become over-extended and the latter has atrophied . . . To restore a proper balance between city and rural life is perhaps the greatest task in front of modern man.

—E.F. Schumacher[1]

This book is about the *future of work* and its implications for people, organizations, nations and governments, and especially for India aka Bharat. Since the future of work is an emergent phenomenon, I use it as a provisional construct and refer to it in italics throughout this book. While the discourse on the *future of work* can be vast, in this book, I have chosen to deal with three broad aspects of it: i) How digital technologies impact work, people and organizations, ii) Why and how flexibility—as operationalized through remote/hybrid work models—will be the new currency in the world of work, and iii) How, by carefully shaping and fast-forwarding the *future of work* in adopting flexible work arrangements, we can create more inclusive employment for rural India.

If the thoughts proposed here can inform policymaking at state and national levels, I believe we can take work to the people, prevent migration to the cities, develop rural economies and unleash the massive potential of our vast human capital.

No doubt, many thinkers, policymakers and the government are actively engaged with these very issues. A lot has already been discussed and written on these topics. Through this book, I aim to join the overall discourse on accelerating growth in India through more inclusive human capital strategies. In this sense, I will perhaps be adding to or even repeating what others have said before. The only non-mainstream idea I propose in this book is how flexibility—especially new work models, like remote and hybrid work—can be game-changing and transformational for India. These work models are discussed largely at corporate firms—that too with mixed reactions. I think it's time to raise the discussion to the national policymaking levels. I argue that these and other forms of work flexibility can be cornerstones of our national strategies for inclusive employment, bridging the gap between Bharat (rural) and India (urban).

Bharat, in this book, is used only to differentiate rural from urban India, and I have no intention of joining any political debate around the use of these two names for India.

The twin forces of digitalization and demographic shifts, accelerated by the lessons learnt from the recent Covid-19 pandemic, set a unique and historic stage for greater flexibility at the individual, organizational and national levels. And we should not miss this wonderful opportunity.

Overall, please expect to find some new perspectives on how we can shape and steer the *future of work* for India and be more selective and discriminating about what to adopt and what to avoid from the many offerings that the *future of work* will present. India has a never-before opportunity to leapfrog, not only in technology but also in work models. We must not suffer the evolving (largely West-led) discourse around the *future of work*. We must create and shape our own.

Let's begin with what has been accomplished and what more needs to be done.

Now that India is well poised to be the world's third-largest economy in GDP terms, our attention has turned even more urgently to greater inclusive growth, and rightly so. The good news is that we have made major strides in terms of financial inclusion. The results are here to see: cumulatively, 500 million Jan-Dhan accounts (government initiative for opening a basic savings bank account for the unbanked person) have been opened, taking India's bankable count to 80 per cent[2] of its population. With this, it has become possible now to do a direct transfer of benefits to people, who earlier used to lose a large share of their legitimate dues to intermediaries. A massive sum of approximately \$427 billion has reached the right beneficiaries cumulatively since the start of the scheme in 2013.[3] Another exemplary step in financial inclusion has been India's development and deployment of a massively successful Unified Payments Interface (UPI) payment platform, an instant real-time payment system to facilitate inter-bank transactions through mobile phones. More than 300 million Indians have started using this vast, seamless and easy-to-use mode for financial transactions.[4] All these have been pioneering measures pushing the agenda of financial inclusion in India. Coupled with the growth in the penetration of Internet and mobile phone services, millions in rural India have now moved formally into the mainstream economy with never-experienced-before ease of carrying out financial transactions.

But what about human capital inclusion?

As of 2023, India's working-age population (aged fifteen to sixty-four) numbered around 951 million. This is likely to grow to a staggering 1.04 billion by 2030.[5] On the other hand, the labour-force participation rate (LFPR) in India is low, at about 57.9.[6] LFPR refers to percentage of the working-age population that is currently employed or seeking employment. Extrapolating this trend, we come to the frightening probability that as many as 400 million (close to 42 per cent of the working-age population estimated for 2030) will not participate in the labour force. That would be one of the largest human capital exclusions in the world. Scary, isn't it? More than the above projections, the magnitude of the task of including such a massive number of working-age population in the labour force in the near future should concern us.

We are faced with a painful paradox: many jobs go a-begging for lack of right people for them, while many people are begging for jobs. This is a systemic failure. The plumbing between education and skills, skills and employability, and employability and accessibility to decent jobs is broken and needs a serious overhaul. Admittedly, this is a huge task and there are no silver bullets. Efforts like the National Education Policy 2020, the proposed labour-law reforms and the widespread skilling programmes, including those led by the National Skill Development Corporation, and the various employment-creation programmes by the central and state governments are all in the right direction. But they don't seem to add up the same way the financial inclusion measures have done.

Looking from the ground up, the dots still need to connect, and one senses the lack of a cohesive strategy in getting them to connect.

On the one hand, creating enough jobs for everyone and providing equal opportunity to all to make them accessible to everyone continues to be the hardest challenge for India. On the other hand, the *future of work*, ushered in by new digital technologies, comes with a significant impact on job creation. The progress of new-age technologies like artificial intelligence (AI), machine learning (ML), robotics, 3-D printing, blockchain and augmented reality/virtual reality (AR/VR) is irreversible. These and other technologies— often known as Industry 4.0—will mean fewer jobs and not more, at a unit level. Historically, the introduction of new technologies has always created immediate job losses but long-term job gains through a process of painful adjustment and re-skilling. An estimate by the consulting firm McKinsey says India is faced with the unenviable task of creating 90 million non-farm jobs during 2020–30 (even as some forecasts peg the requirement at an incredible 200 million).[7]

Hence, India must be circumspect about adopting these technologies blindly. We must create an *Indian version of the future of work* and shape our future on our terms. While this is a big ask, it provides us the much-needed context to think about what we can do to address our employment issues.

While the global discourse on the *future of work* is currently focused mainly on the use/abuse of technologies such as AI and ML, we need to go beyond this and explore other aspects of the *future of work* that can be leveraged to India's advantage.

Let us start by looking at some of the key opportunities (especially accentuated by our recent and exceptional tryst with the Covid-19 virus) that can be used to address the India-specific challenge of providing sustainable livelihoods to the millions of our folk now trapped in Bharat (rural and semi-urban India) and mainstream them into rising urban India. In the grander scheme of things, I believe that if we thoughtfully shape the *future of work* and steer it on our terms, we can not only unleash our vast human capital but also leapfrog India into being the capital of human capital globally. In this book we will specifically discuss the top ten future trends and opportunities that I believe should inform our thinking as well as policymaking, both at the firm and societal levels:

i)   Digitalization of work and workspaces.
ii) New opportunities for working from anywhere and for hybrid work.
iii) Work and life expectations of the rising youth (often referred to as Gen Z).
iv) Flexibility as the edifice of the new-age work ethos.
v)   Rise of a distinct preference for autonomy and self-direction.
vi) Knock-on effects of the changing preferences of the next-gen workforce on people management and leadership styles.
vii) Growing and stifling urban congestion.
viii) Rising carbon emissions.
ix) Growing commute challenges.
x)   Misery of migration for rural youth.

These are not just trends, but imperatives of the emerging future. If they are understood and handled well, and in time, India can be catapulted on to the global stage as a truly advanced society and not just an as an advanced economy.

Unfortunately, however, we do not have well-established and universally accepted metrics to measure what constitutes a holistic, advanced economy or society. In recent times, tired of using the gross domestic product (GDP) as the sole measure of economic success, think-tanks and nations are proposing alternative measures. The human development index (HDI) proposed by the United Nations Development Programme, the inclusive development index proposed by the World Economic Forum and, interestingly, the gross national happiness index, initially proposed by the government of Bhutan, are some of the emerging measures being considered to determine the degree of holistic development of societies. In this context, it will be interesting to explore human capital inclusion as another important measure.

Let me outline what I mean by human capital inclusion. In my opinion, it should refer to proactive actions by the state, by firms and other institutions to seek out talent without any bias against location, background, gender, physical disabilities, sexual orientation, age, etc. It also means reducing or removing the barriers to acquisition of skills and knowledge, as well as to employment, for the rural and underprivileged communities. In summary, equal opportunities and barrier-free access to education, skills, employment and livelihoods to all sections of society constitute human capital inclusion. In this book, we will explore this concept further and explain why human capital inclusion should be viewed as the cause of growth and not as its consequence.

The most striking feature of the story of an otherwise rising India is its inability to build inclusive employment and livelihoods for its rural population. Our access to formal employment, education, healthcare, lifestyle and many other vital aspects of what constitutes quality of life, is distinctly skewed towards a few urban centres, while the vast rural hinterland struggles for a level playing field.

In this book, I address the challenge of building an inclusive human capital framework for India that can bridge the gap between India and Bharat. This book will also outline and discuss how some non-mainstream ideas regarding jobs, work and models of employment, when adopted at scale, can create this much-needed inclusion.

My central proposition is that *how we work determines who gets to work*.

Consider the following:

i)   If work can happen only in predefined 'offices'/sites, usually located in the big cities, then those who cannot come to these cities will not be able to participate in the workforce.

ii) Additionally, if decent work is given preferentially only to city-bred, English-speaking youth from elite schools, then a whole lot of talented rural and semi-urban folk will forever remain outside the mainstream of employment.

iii) Even within cities, if in-person co-location within defined premises is the mandate (despite the technology available at scale for work to be delivered digitally from anywhere), then many who cannot be present in person at the workplace will lose out.

iv) Fixed hours, regimented schedules and 'presenteeism', in return for a so-called long-term career, tend to keep sections of women, people with disabilities, senior citizens and several other talented people out of the workforce.

v)   If managers and leaders continue to make work 'suck', as the twenty-somethings say often, then many self-respecting individuals will exclude themselves from such work and will prefer self-employment even if it is not sustainable. In this context, it does not come as a surprise that Randstad's Workmonitor 2022 report states that 63 per cent of the Indian workforce would rather be unemployed than unhappy in a job.[8]

Thus, how we work, where we work, whom we work for, whom we hire, what technologies we use to deliver work, how we design our employment contracts and, most importantly, how we treat and lead people, determine who can participate and thrive in the workforce. In a way, our restrictive and 'stuck-in-the-industrial-era' work models and leadership styles are denying and delaying inclusion, depriving many of opportunities to get to and flourish at work.

If we change how we work, more people will get to formal work.

The recent pandemic and the rapid advances in digital technologies used at the workplace comprise a momentous watershed in humanity's ongoing tryst with work and work forms. It will be a pity if we fail to learn the lessons from these twin forces and 'return to office' (as they say), as do alcoholics to the pub after a few days of induced sobriety.

A major lesson the pandemic has taught us is that people do not have to always go to work; work too can go to where people are. We witnessed, through an unexpectedly large, global-scale work experiment (as millions worked from home), that remote work can be an equal and viable alternative to office-based work. Remote work, at the massive scale we saw this time, was not about some privileged few working from home. We saw it working for millions of tech workers across countries . I believe this opens the single-largest opportunity to bridge the growing gap between India and Bharat. It goes without saying that if we decide not to bridge this gap and continue to take people to where work is, which is mostly to massive office buildings and worksites in select urban centres, we will continue to have to contend with the horrors of migration. Remember the shock of watching on national television our country cousins walking hundreds of kilometres back home from big urban clusters like the national capital region in May 2020?[9]

I argue that if we can build a robust ecosystem for nurturing remote work as a viable alternative to office-based work, the nation will create stronger human capital inclusion, leading to greater employment and greater employability. Remote work and all its mutants— work from home, work from anywhere, work from neighbourhood co-location hubs, work during staycations or all work essentially untethered from a fixed location— can open up new models of employment. Such flexible models of employment will increase inclusive access to jobs for millions, especially in rural India.

In summary, I am presenting a case for changing the way we work, thereby unleashing the human capital of India and driving greater inclusion, especially for our rural people, and accelerating the convergence of Bharat with India.

Let me now outline how I have dealt with this subject and evolved the arguments in this book through its various chapters.

In Chapter 1, I begin by briefly examining the history of work and outlining how the present-day office is a relatively recent phenomenon. It's only in the last 300 years or so that we started going to a place specially designated for work. For centuries before that, work was not about a place to go to. Work that started in forests and fields moved over time to homes, backyards and village hubs, and stayed there for a long time. A closer examination of the history of work will also tell us that work had the best impact on people when it was largely untethered from a designated place and when people had the autonomy to choose both their place and time of work. Imperialism and industrialization both forced work to be concentrated in defined places so that control and supervision could be effective. For true agency and intrapreneurship—fountainheads for unleashing the potential of human capital—we need to turn a new chapter in the history of work and shape the *future of work,* unshackling work as well as workers from the restrictive practices of the past.

In Chapter 2, I discuss how Covid-19 was not just another pandemic. It has had epoch-making characteristics, changing the course of history on many fronts. This crisis has presented us with a unique opportunity to break away from the past and change for ever many aspects of our personal, professional and organizational lives. While the pandemic took us back in time and returned us to homes from where we worked, we are continuing to waver on this front. Our response to work during and after the Covid-19 crisis has been, at best, an emergency response to the threat from a virus. Initially, we went back to our homes for fear of the virus spreading. As that fear subsided, we ran back to our offices. Again, as another wave of the pandemic loomed, we flipped back. Currently, we think we need both: the bonhomie of the office and the freedom of choosing our own space to do serious work. Hence, we have settled for what is now called hybrid work. But changes in modes of working are only one of the many far-reaching consequences of the Covid-19 pandemic. In this chapter, we will examine what the other effects of this and other similar crises (climate change?) will be, and how we should cope with the *future of work*.

In Chapter 3, I discuss the emergent global discourse on the *future of work*. We will also examine its relevance to India in its current stage of socio-economic evolution. The discussion on the *future of work* is largely led by Western narratives, with consulting companies dominating the discourse.[10]

Further, most of the discussion on the *future of work* is centred on two big themes: first, the impact of automation and emerging technologies of AI and ML on work and jobs; second, the emergence of new models of work and the demand for flexibility, leading to greater adoption of remote work and hybrid work models.

In this chapter, I discuss how India must shape the *future of work* to suit its unique needs and not indiscriminately ape the Western models. Again, this is not one of those overly patriotic and parochial nationalist views, but a well-considered opinion on what to take from the West and where to 'adapt' the learnings of the West to best fit our unique needs.

Rich, with much bigger welfare and social security budgets and much smaller populations to support, Western and advanced nations have to contend with rather different implications of the threats of automation than do highly populated and emerging economies like India.

India needs many more jobs, period. Automation meant to solely eliminate jobs needs to be evaluated carefully. Automation for improvement in efficiency, productivity and value-add is understandable, for it creates new job opportunities. But the choice of automation either because it is the new shiny object on the horizon or merely to join the bandwagon of the so-called advanced nations is a trap and may be counterproductive for India. We examine in this chapter many India-specific factors around demographics, labour-force participation rates, the rise of tier-two towns, etc. Following a close analysis of India's opportunities, we discuss some potential steps that can be taken to shape the *future of work,* specifically in the unique context of India, where it will demand very high levels of flexibility in employment policies, governance structures and people management practices.

Chapter 4 focuses on the rise of the remote and flexible work order. There are three levels at which flexibility is emerging to be the preferred design feature in how we work, whom we work with and where we work.

i)   At the individual level, flexibility in work models is showing up in the breakdown of the conventional career models, giving place to a preference for several newer models, like part-time, contract, freelance, gig, on-call, telework, telecommuting, remote work, work from home, work from anywhere, etc.

ii)   At the team level, we are now seeing more fluid and agile teams, networks, self-managed teams and hybrid work teams.

iii) At the organizational level, we are now required to cope with many new forms of flexibility by reimagining workspaces, breaking down cubicles and creating collaborative lounge spaces. The office of the future will be more suitable for socializing than for serious work. With the shifting role of the office, the ease of working remotely and adoption of other work models, flexibility will increase manifold. And this will not be so for the IT sector alone.

In Chapter 5, I bust the myth that *remote work is only for the IT sector and white-collar jobs*. In this chapter, I explain how sectors like fast-moving consumer goods (FMCG), pharma and healthcare, construction and projects, building work, domains like manufacturing and agriculture, and professions like sales, quality and lab testing have started using remote work. Of course, with 'tech' appended to many traditional sectors—like 'edtech', 'healthtech', 'foodtech', 'fintech', etc.—we have whole new domains that have opened up new jobs that can be done from anywhere.

In this chapter, I look at case studies from both traditional and new-age companies to understand the new possibilities of doing work in the least expected places: like the driving of forklifts by someone who is not at the construction site, the performance of surgeries without the surgeon being at the operating theatre, the testing of drug samples outside of the laboratory, or the tilling of farms without the farmer being in the field. The power of technology has made not only IT and white-collar jobs tech-enabled, and therefore free from locational compulsions, but has also untethered jobs for traditional workers in manufacturing, construction, etc. The pandemic has spawned many innovations, pushing the limits of technology to make even industrial work as contact-less as possible. The lines between manual/physical work, IT and machine-enabled work are blurring constantly. Industry 4.0 technologies, such as the industrial Internet of things (IoT), connected manufacturing and smart factories are becoming prominent.

Overall, the story of human evolution vis-a-vis work is one of a constant endeavour to reduce physical effort by humans. Through tools, machines, computers, and now 'cyber-physical' systems, down different eras, we have been trying to make our tasks easier, more efficient and less strenuous. This evolution will continue even as it poses significant challenges to providing sustainable employment to our vast population. It is about time we changed our thinking, which is still rooted in the early industrial era, centred on the need to assemble people physically in designated workplaces.

In Chapter 6, I discuss the opportunities that the *future of work* presents and how they can help us unleash our vast human capital, beyond what the current initiatives around inclusive growth are enabling. Economists and public-policy thinkers have rightly pointed out that sheer growth by itself may not benefit all sections of society. Hence, there is a need for proactive interventions by the state to ensure that the benefits of growth reach everyone— especially the poor and the underprivileged. Known broadly as inclusive growth, it calls out for the need to ensure distributive justice and include people in enjoying the benefits of growth more equitably. Present-day India is pursuing this through several proven financial inclusion measures. The direct transfer of benefits and platforms like the UPI are great accomplishments towards inclusive growth. But all this assumes that growth happens first and that we must then ensure that the benefits of growth reach all. In this chapter, I take a slightly different view and argue that human capital inclusion must precede growth and be treated as a growth accelerator *ex-ante*. Thus, we must be more inclusive regarding our human capital, both during its formation and its eventual deployment. This will shift our approach, and we might be better off to have thought of inclusion before growth than after.

In Chapter 7, I turn our attention to Bharat, since this is where lies the vast untapped reservoir of the human capital of India, waiting to be included. While Bharat *sounds* more like a politically inclined expression than anything else, I think it provides a unique construct to contrast the relative prosperity and privileges of a few large urban centres of India with the vast rural regions of India playing catch-up all the time. Survey figures for 2021 show that 35.39 per cent of India's population resides in urban cities while 64.61 per cent resides in rural areas.[11] In this chapter, I outline the challenges Bharat faces in integrating with mainstream big-city India in three key areas: i) Access to employable skills, ii) Formal employment, and iii) Access to reliable broadband Internet. In this chapter, I discuss how Bharat—the relatively underdeveloped talent territory of India—is the next future of India. The good news is that Bharat is changing rapidly. For one, consumption of goods and services is on the rise in rural India. Whether it is fast-moving consumer goods (FMCG), automobiles or demat accounts for stock trading, it is customers from rural and semi-urban markets that are driving unprecedented growth in India. For example, you will find a surprisingly large number of luxury cars in smaller cities such as Surat and Ludhiana.[12] These are all heartening changes. However, they need to be widespread and not restricted to a small, privileged elite in these towns, where the vast majority struggles to find decent jobs and access to reasonable schools and hospitals. The burgeoning growth of Bharat will see a quantum leap if we can create enough jobs in the smaller towns. We must take work to where people are and not force them to migrate to the big cities.

In Chapter 8, I examine how we can take work to rural India by adopting some of the unique gifts of the *future of work*. By embracing flexibility—which the *future of work* demands—and avoiding job-eliminating technologies, we can shape the *future of work* to suit the needs of both growing Bharat and ascendant India. I also look at the pioneering examples set by companies like Zoho, Tata Steel, Air India and Hindustan Lever in taking jobs to villages and small towns. To understand what happened (some of which effects continue to this day) to Bharat during the Covid-19 pandemic, I spoke with 200 employees of a large global IT firm who had been working from across thirty small towns ever since the pandemic. Probing their experience of over three years of carrying their work to smaller towns and living away from the big cities, I found that it brought them many benefits. Of course, there were downsides too.

Another way of taking work to rural India is to intentionally set up work facilities in small towns. In this context, I review the exemplary Tenkasi model of rural job creation by Zoho (the $1 billion made-in-India IT firm). Yes, we have some way to go in bridging the gap between urban and rural India. Bharat must be ready to receive jobs from India. At the same time, jobs must go to Bharat so that the small towns can receive more by way of benefits.

Remote work and several other reforms in how we work, whom we include, invite and facilitate to join work, and how we train, treat and prepare the workforce of the future will be key in bringing about the change we so badly want. No one is better positioned to take the lead than firms themselves. Small and medium firms in India have a unique opportunity to build inclusive organizations that are flexible, fair and conscious of their responsibility to create jobs, especially for rural India.

In Chapter 9, I examine the demographic dividend of India and direct our thoughts on what will it mean to engage and lead the next generation of the emerging workforce, popularly known as Gen Z. I will outline the generational shifts, present the Western conceptualization of the *future of work* and discuss what could be different for India. India's Gen Z has its own unique characteristics and needs. Our leaders must address their needs differently from the way they addressed the needs of the previous generations of workforce and engage with Gen Z in a way that is relevant in the Indian context. Gen Z will shape the *future of work* and leadership by demanding higher levels of self-determination and flexibility.

In Chapter 10, I move from macro- to micro-analysis and discuss how to build flexible and fair organizations for the future. As we discuss how to ready India Inc. for the future, we notice the critical roles of three important actors: 1) Boards of directors and chief executive officers, 2) Chief human resource officers, and 3) Managers. If you take a closer look, you will find that many of our corporate boards, CEOs and HR leaders—the primary movers when it comes to unleashing human potential—are stuck in the 'dreary desert sand of dead habit', to use the words of the famous poet Rabindranath Tagore. Of course, the fourth leg of the equation, the 'employee' must learn to match autonomy with accountability. Consistent with the overall spirit of the book, I will avoid doling out the 'seven-practices-for-guaranteed-success' type of cookie-cutter solutions. Instead, a critical evaluation of current approaches and our anticipations of what needs to change will be discussed. The hope is that the important stakeholders in building an inclusive human capital ecosystem are persuaded, provoked and stimulated to act differently and better.

Having established the importance of flexibility in the previous chapters, I go on to ask some important questions about the on-ground feasibility of flexibility in Chapter 11. We know that there are many views against flexibility. The old school of discipline and command and control continues to hang heavily over the world of work, and perhaps will continue into the near future. Many questions are raised, essentially challenging the so-called 'too liberal' ideas of flexibility. Some of these questions are about the digital divide as well as trust and whether workers will cheat when they work remotely. The questions also pertain to how managers will manage a remote workforce, how one can build a company culture without people coming together in person, and more.

There will be these strong pushbacks, and there are no foolproof answers at this time, just as there were none when man transitioned from the cave to agriculture and then to industry. At the same time, it is also worth recognizing that from the vantage point of the present, the future almost always looks threatening. When we collectively dwell on these issues, we will realize that the path to flexibility must be paved slowly and patiently, and it will take a few decades, if not longer. But many of the challenges are not insurmountable.

In the final chapter (Chapter 12), I outline how we must have a national strategy to build a whole new ecosystem to unleash the vast human capital of India based on the principles of flexibility.

We must ask ourselves: If a well-entrenched and leading firm based in Boston (USA) could trust an unknown firm in Bengaluru (then Bangalore) way back in 1980 (think of Infosys) to deliver work from India, why can't this Bengaluru firm trust its people in Belagavi (formerly Belgaum) to deliver work from their home town? How did we move work successfully from Houston to Hyderabad, and why are we struggling to move it from Hyderabad to Hissar?

In this last chapter, I will discuss and propose how an ecosystem for remote and flexible work can be built in our small towns. Internationally, many countries, and sometimes small towns themselves, have already put in place incentives to attract remote workers, which can trigger several knock-on effects for the all-round development of the local economies. Both India and Bharat can learn from these examples.

Working out of offices—the present default mode of work—is a recent phenomenon in the history and evolution of work forms. To make these offices attractive and somewhat useful, we built a whole ecosystem of urban centres, roads, metros, parking spaces and restaurants, and invested in building well-designed offices that can attract, host, feed and entertain employees, in the hope that a lot of productive work will happen. Some work happened and a lot of habits were created, which made us 'creatures of the office' addicting us to treating office as the default place of work.

As we anticipate and ready ourselves for a *future of work* that is not anchored in a place called office—and especially if we want to create and offer jobs in rural areas on the back of a new work order—we need to build a fresh, new ecosystem. Much like our cities got built, our small towns must be equipped to host and facilitate delivery of productive work safely and conveniently. This will mean a whole new ecosystem—which I will discuss (backed by the research I did during the pandemic).

As I conclude the book, I peep into the future—marked by climate change and many daily disruptions, which require people to connect more using virtual media. Gen Z and Gen Alpha's preferences for treating virtual as the new real, and advances in immersive video technologies, will further accelerate the rise of remote work. Today's children will, in the future, work in completely new job types that don't yet exist.[13] At the intersection of swiftly changing technologies and societal as well as generational changes, work, workforce and workspaces—the three pillars of the *future of work*—are bound to undergo an orbit shift. We have no choice but to adjust, modify and adapt the way work so that more of us can be at work and enjoy it at the same time.

To sum up, this book aims to persuade firms and policymakers to shape the *future of work* for India's unique needs instead of merely suffering it as it unfolds. As I give the final touches to this book, the world is moving on, choosing to ignore the lessons from the pandemic that shook us just three years ago. Strong forces of habit, our long-held (and unexamined) beliefs and, more importantly, our inability to discern the opportunities underlying the evolving course of the *future of work* are pushing us back to preserving the status quo. This book joins a minority of writers and thinkers who are pleading for greater discrimination when it comes to what we adopt and what we reject from the *future of work* possibilities.

We are at a significant inflection point in steering the course of the history of work. By seizing the opportunities that digital technologies present, while being mindful of the unique needs of India, we can leapfrog India's work models to an exciting new era, where work travels to people and people don't travel to work. And that will be game changing.

I sincerely hope you will see this book both as a passionate plea and a reasoned argument for why we should adopt flexible work models (including remote work) to unleash the vast human capital of India.

1

Work through the Arc of Time

Humankind, it seems, is not yet ready to claim its collective pension. Understanding why requires recognizing that our relationship with work is far more interesting and involved than most traditional economists would have us believe.

—James Suzman[1]

David Foster Wallace, renowned American author and novelist, narrated an interesting story in his commencement speech at Kenyon College, the famous private liberal arts college in Gambier, Ohio, USA, in 2005. In this tale, an old fish casually asks a young fish swimming along, 'How's the water?' This innocuous question, however, left the young fish perturbed. 'What the hell is water?' he wondered. The familiar tends to make us this way; the 'most obvious, important realities are often the ones that are hardest to see and talk about'.[2] Such has been our

1

relationship with work in our offices. We can no longer separate work from the office.

The pandemic, however, has to some extent upended this. While it is nearly impossible to use the words 'pandemic' and 'positive' in the same sentence, the fact remains that this dreadful experience has offered us several invaluable gifts. It has given us a once-in-a-lifetime opportunity to press the reset button for work, has showed us the possibility of making our work lives more flexible, and has made us think about purpose more often than before.

The full implication of why the pandemic has compelled us to reimagine work, however, lies in the annals of history. As they say, to know your future you must know your past. It is important, therefore, to begin with understanding what really humanity's tryst with work has been over the centuries and what sense work and, particularly, workplaces have made to people over time. Looking at the canvas of the history of work, we soon realize that workplaces (offices), as we see them in their current avatar, have never been the default setting for work, as we have made them now.

Early man, of course, was a hunter-gatherer, a nomad shifting from place to place simply to find food. Surviving at that time meant not getting tied down to a single place where people would work. In his book *Work: A History of How We Spend Our Time*, Thomas Suzman, whom we have quoted above, explains beautifully how the early foraging tribes the Ju/hoansi 'Bushmen' of southern Africa's Kalahari deserts, who still lived as hunter-gatherers up to the late twentieth century, had a different view of work until the European colonizers ambushed them and taught them, by brute force, the virtues of hard work. Suzman says: 'But we now know that hunter-gatherers like the Ju/'hoansi did not live constantly on the edge of starvation.

Rather, they were usually well nourished; lived longer than people in most farming societies; rarely worked more than fifteen hours a week, and spent the bulk of their time at rest and leisure.'

It is estimated that for close to 95 per cent of the 3,00,000 years or so of the history of *Homo sapiens*, people remained nomads, worked as little as required and out of any place that suited them. However, due to the vast uncertainties and vagaries of nature, and the seasonality of food availability, people had to 'settle down' to ensure food security for themselves. This started the early organization of work and settlements. It took several centuries after that for work to look the way we see it today.

The *Encyclopedia Britannica* gives us a description of work in 5000 BP (before present), which looks very close to what it is today. The authors of the section on the origins of agriculture talk about a new town, Ur, in Sumer, which is now in modern Iraq (earlier Mesopotamia) and lay between the Tigris and Euphrates rivers. They write:

> It has been estimated that at Ur, a large town covering some 50 acres (20 hectares) within a cultivated **enclave, there were 10,000 animals confined in sheepfolds and stables, of which 3,000 were slaughtered each year.** Ur's population **of about 6,000 people included a** labor force of 2,500 who annually cultivated 3,000 acres of land (**some 1,200** hectares), leaving an equal amount of land fallow. The workforce included storehouse recorders, work foremen, overseers, and harvest **supervisors, as well as** laborers.[3]

Look at how soon settling down in a place or anchoring in a town started breeding hierarchy and supervision, even in the early days of organized work!

It took several more centuries for this settling down to advance and create enough predictable surpluses of food and fodder, unlike in the previous nomadic era. But with this came organization and class systems.

However, for a long time, there was no clear separation between home and work. In ancient India (sixth century BC) there arose a class of traders and guilds. Artisans produced excellent goods and crafts. The artisan manufactured goods by hand in a small shed in his house or at a small shop located nearby, which enabled him to oversee his household throughout the day. Work and leisure overlapped in the lives of urban artisans. Work patterns tended to be punctuated by leisure breaks. During the slow periods, workers enjoyed singing, drinking and gambling in their local communities. Artisans often took time off to attend wrestling matches, horse races and performances by travelling musicians and acrobats.

If you closely examine the historical records, it is also evident that the craftsmen, not being tied down to the narrow confines of workspaces, felt free and performed to their potential. Work not only provided them with a living but also a strong identity, and they took great pride in their reputation as craftsmen. Michael Kimmel, in his book *Manhood in America*, speaks of the 'heroic artisan' as an archetype: 'The artisanal ideal was that of an honest toiler, unafraid of hard work, proud of and happy with his craftsmanship and self-reliance.'[4]

In the first 1700 years of this millennium, work was organized variously, often in and around farms as well as inland and maritime trade. Early manufacturing was done by cottage- and village-based industries. During this time, people enjoyed mobility and freedom to integrate work with life; and the higher classes enjoyed greater autonomy and agency than the lower classes.

However, by the mid-eighteenth century, and with the advent of industrialization, the course of work changed dramatically. The need for standardization, mass production and large-scale record-keeping forced people to congregate at factories and in offices. The earliest formal office building in the Western world is reckoned to be the Old Admiralty Office in London set up in 1726. This was followed by the offices of the East India Company, in 1729. It was, however, in the nineteenth century, when clerks started working in dark, cramped places that we saw the rise of what really became the proto-office. The modern office evolved from these 'counting houses' of the mid-nineteenth century, along with the emergence of white-collar workers.

With the rapid increase in offices in the early twentieth century, for the first time in history, people began to labour in 'cube farms' and were stuck next to each other for long hours in six-by-six cubicles. As Nikil Saval, an American writer, editor and political activist, points out, 'It is no coincidence that the word "cubicle" is rarely, if ever, mentioned in dignified solitude; instead, it is prefaced with some inevitable epithet: "windowless" or "dreary".'[5] It also turned white-collar work into numbing, repetitive labour, and work started to feel like drudgery because the old factory model was merely continued in the modern offices. Twisting the famous words of the French philosopher Rousseau, one can say: man is born free, but he is everywhere in cubicles. Even the best intentions of planners and architects fell short of producing a happy environment for the workers. Recognizing the need to make offices more 'liveable', Larkin, the famous soap manufacturer of the late nineteenth century, engaged the well-known architect firm Frank Lloyd Wright to design their state-of-the-art headquarters in Buffalo, New York. A distinguishing feature of the building was the central court with a roof that let in natural light. Even though, physically speaking, the Larkin building was a huge advancement over the dingy work areas of the time, it was menacing for other reasons; not only did the numbing work remain the same, but there were managers spying to see that the work was being done efficiently. It was almost as if the building was designed for surveillance. Clearly, the developments around offices and factories in the industrial era worsened the human experience with work.[6]

For a while now, workers have been made to believe in and celebrate the intrinsic virtues of 'assembling' at a place called an office or factory as a daily chore. However, the lived experiences in these physical spaces have been diverse. While conventional wisdom had it that offices are critical to productivity, to culture, and in winning the war for talent, workers in these buildings began to experience growing ennui and disenchantment with work itself. For several generations since, people have often viewed work as oppressive and stultifying and have nursed a common desire to liberate themselves from the drudgery of it.

Of course, if you look at work as a construct, you are likely to see it as a burden or as a blessing, depending on the period of history and the part of the world you are in. Seen through the lens of Western historians, work has often been regarded as a weight to be carried. The genesis of this may lie at the beginning of civilization itself, with God's curse on Adam, one that compelled him to work to earn his living in light of the original sin. '*By the sweat of your brow you will eat your food until you return to the ground, since from it you were taken* (Genesis 3:19).' Adam was thus destined to earn his food the hard way, sweating in the fields from dawn to dusk until he returned to the ground himself, dead and buried. Come to think of it, the so-called 'fairy tales' also present work as something deplorable—whether it was Cinderella, who had to undertake menial tasks, or Jack, who exchanged the hard work at the farm for some magic seeds. The dream of escaping work seemed to be a common thread that ran through many lives. Think of the modern-day remnant of this idea of work as pain. For example, the French word for work, 'travail', means more than just effort. It also connotes suffering. No wonder the French protested recently when asked to work beyond the age of sixty-two!

On a separate note, it is interesting to see how work was treated, and sometimes glorified, especially by religion. In the sixteenth and seventeenth centuries, the European world saw the rise of the Protestant work ethic. The proponents of Calvinism reversed the previous dark and damning understanding of work, and for the first time work started to get celebrated. People were urged to create an economic surplus, laying the foundations of a mercantile history. Work was at this time synonymous with identity, meaning esteem and self-actualization. Calvinists considered the selection of an occupation and its pursuit for profit a religious duty. They worked in their chosen occupations with an attitude of service to God and associated success at work with the likelihood of being one of God's elects. Industrialization, of course, changed all of this, as we saw earlier.

Cut to India and the Eastern world, where in contrast to the West, in the early times, work lay at the intersection between dharma and karma and acquired both materialistic and spiritual significance at the same time. The ancient Hindu understanding of 'self-actualization' was far ahead of Maslow's, not just in chronology but also in content.

People with various skills, trades and occupations were celebrated for their dedication and professionalism. Over time, though, the concept of work degenerated and a rigid caste system took root. In the caste hierarchy, the work of the upper castes was positioned as intrinsically superior. It was marked by greater volition and agency, and was believed to be serving a higher purpose. However, to those at the lower end of the spectrum—who were often commanded, controlled and ordered around—work became synonymous with drudgery. Thus, depending on where you found yourself in the caste hierarchy, you either enjoyed your work or suffered it.

As we look at the evolution of work through the prism of time, it is evident that the experience and meaning of work have evolved at the interface between the location of work and the flexibility and agency workers had. Whenever work was done voluntarily, with autonomy, freedom, discretion, self-direction and, above all, at a place of the worker's choice, it was enjoyed and was seen as a source of meaning and significance. On the other hand, whenever it was controlled, directed, forced or tied to externally driven rewards and punishments, it was experienced as alienation, ennui, drudgery and exploitation.

Humanity's tryst with work has brought us to a point where we are questioning more seriously than ever before the relevance of regimented, location-fixated and time-bound work, especially after the Covid-19 pandemic. In essence, we are at an inflection point in the evolution of our engagement with work. Through this journey, while paid and salaried work gave people their livelihood, steady income, power, influence, identity and esteem in varying degrees, it also trapped people into submitting to the increasingly oppressive demands of their workplaces and their owners/managers.

The recent pandemic, and just the sheer zeitgeist of our times, have unleashed three big forces that I believe will accelerate our quest for a new equation with work: i) Rapid digitalization and new uses of AI and ML technologies, ii) Dramatic demographic shifts, and iii) Increased use of social media for activism, protests and leaderless, autonomous and networked movements, reminding us of the Latin adage *vox populi, vox dei*.

Digitalization: With a number of immersive technologies on the anvil and the use of extended reality (XR), new forms of communication and collaboration are set to change the way we work. We are increasingly going to see several tools that will relieve the monotony of video meetings and improve the limited functionality of messaging apps. There seems to be an irresistible quest to create the virtual as an alternative to the real. Major technology providers are increasingly making their tools more sophisticated in this direction. Recent developments such as the video-conferencing platform Zoom's partnering with Oculus to create functionality for virtual reality (VR) meetings, Microsoft's announcement of 'Mesh for Microsoft Teams' to create advanced immersive holographic experiences, and Cisco's unveiling of the Webex Hologram, a hybrid work-collaboration tool powered by augmented reality, will mark the next significant developments making the virtual closer to real. XR technologies will have a very transformative impact on how we work and will set the stage for a new world of work, much like factories did in the eighteenth century.

Demographic shifts: What is also likely to intensify the shift to hybrid and remote work is the demographic shift to

Gen Z and Gen Alpha (over time, though), especially in the ascendant and emerging economies of India, Asia, Africa and Latin America. The youth of the future will prioritize freedom over security, flexibility over stability, and agency and autonomy over direction and instruction. Work preferences are bound to see a shift. With it will come the necessity to establish a new way of working that bypasses the traditional bureaucratic and hierarchical organization model. With democratic tendencies taking stronger root, there will be without doubt a need for self-managed teams.

Social media: While social media has been on the rise for a while, the forced lockdowns of the pandemic intensified its usage manifold. A large-scale survey revealed a sharp increase (about 20 per cent) in worldwide social media usage from before the pandemic.[7]

TikTok is one of the fastest-growing social media apps in the United States and is especially popular with younger digital-native audiences.[8] It has a massive use base of over 100 million and is growing manifold.

The free channels of Facebook, X, Instagram, YouTube, TikTok, etc., have now turned out to be massive tools in the hands of people who want to have their say on matters without any intermediation. A report from Pew Research study of June 2020 says:

> Overall, about one-third of social media users (36%) say they have used sites like Facebook, Twitter and others in the past month to post a picture to show their support for a cause, look up information about rallies or protests happening in their area (35%) or encourage others to take action on issues they regard as important (32%). A smaller share (18%) reports using a hashtag related to a political or social issue on social media.[9]

India too has been seeing a rise in mass protests, largely fuelled by and coordinated through social media. The farmers' protests through 2021, which ultimately lead the government to repeal its farm laws; the gig workers' strike against employers like Urban Company in October 2021, and the bankers' (March 2021) and doctors' strikes (December 2021) are all telling examples of how serious people's movements outside the established and conventional channels are rising, placing the power of action and protest directly in the hands of the people. All this will force governments and managements to revisit their strategies for engaging with people. This has serious implications for the employer–employee interface in the context of work.

These forces will now compel organizations to put people at the centre of work design and to craft human-centric work models.

In the subsequent chapters, we will explore this emerging *future of work* and its huge implications for employment models. Importantly, we will also evaluate whether the *future of work* can unleash new opportunities in the labour market by lowering the locational barriers to work. These issues are even more important in a country like India than in the West, as millions of people in our country need to find meaningful and well-paying jobs over the next decade.

2

The Covid-19 Pandemic

The Beginning of the End of Work as We Know It

There are decades where nothing happens, and there are weeks where decades happen.

—Vladimir Ilyich Lenin[1]

The Covid-19 pandemic seems to have become our new historical dividing line, with BC and AC acquiring new meanings, standing for 'before corona' and 'after corona', respectively. Let us look at work models before and after this event. We can get a good understanding of the changes that the pandemic brought about in the working world by starting with an account of the happenings in China.

It is believed that the coronavirus which triggered the massive pandemic at the end of 2019, leading to a loss of nearly seven million lives across the world up until 2023, started in Wuhan, the Chinese city considered, interestingly, as a 'creative city' by UNESCO. Reckoned as the ground zero of the pandemic, Wuhan put some eleven million people under strict quarantine on 23 January 2020, ahead of the Chinese New Year. This, in turn, set the stage for similar measures in other Chinese cities, in the face of a massive outbreak of the disease.

On the one hand, while the Covid-19-induced lockdowns transformed flourishing business centres into silent towns, the virtual world grew beyond measure. The China News Service published in February 2022 that around 200 million people were working remotely by the end of the Chinese New Year holiday in January 2020.[2] This was a big change. Even if it isn't clear what proportion of the workforce was telecommuting in China before the Covid-19 pandemic, circumstantial evidence suggests that remote working wasn't too prevalent there. In comparison, in the US economy, for example, as much as 43 per cent of workers were working remotely at least some of the time by 2017.[3] It is believed that China's lower work-from-home numbers were a result of its rather conservative work culture and its highly top-down management style. Curiously, not just employee KPIs, but also employee incentive payouts were, until this time, tied closely to employee attendance in a physical space. Given this background, it stands to reason that in a cross-regional survey on global employment trends back in 2018, '85% of surveyed Hong Kong employees had reported that they were required to work at the office during regular office hours with no flexible working options offered.'[4] In any case, the city government was sceptical of teleworking and did not think it would become a mainstream practice any time soon.

The Covid-19 pandemic upended all of that. In fact, the Chinese financial centres of Hong Kong and Shanghai, which employed hundreds of thousands of white-collar office workers, became the frontrunners of the new work-from-home model. This new mode of working was, of course, aided by technology, notably the use of video-conferencing apps such as Tencent's WeChat Work, the Alibaba-owned DingTalk and the US-based Zoom. While everything had seemingly changed, precious little had changed on the ground. The physical clocking in and out of offices was now substituted by the sending of a 'check-in' photo to a virtual group—so much so that in the early days these video-conference call providers were overwhelmed by surges in traffic at work commencement hours, with many users complaining of lag and interruptions. Over time, this turned out to be the least of the concerns in the work-from-home experiment. Alarmingly, many workers complained of invasive bosses who, given their command-control mindset, had little belief in their workers' ability or intention to work unsupervised. Stories emerged in the press of how some companies enforced their regular 9 a.m.-to-8 p.m. work schedule by requiring employees to send their geotagged locations to their offices three times a day.

China in a time machine, ahead of other countries

Interestingly, China, the first country impacted by the pandemic, was also the first to return to office. By the spring of 2020, while employees had begun to re-evaluate their life choices and for the first-time laid emphasis on the freedom to work on their own terms, measures were already being taken by the government to ensure a 'return to normal'. Tech giants such as Alibaba were also insisting that its workforce return to its headquarters.

While the rest of the world continued to be in the throes of the pandemic, China quietly returned to the physical office with its workspaces still designed to support— no marks for guessing—the former ways of working. If anything, it was evident that the shift to remote work was at best an emergency response to the health crisis. That the untethering of work from its traditional location could be leveraged was a lesson that was lost on the world's largest economy, one that was home to some of the world's largest firms.

The one change that made its appearance in different parts of the world was the shift to hybrid work, even though it was also essentially more an ad hoc response to evolving needs, as opposed to a thoughtful choice. However, hybrid work did come as a relief to employees who had been toiling in the '996' (9 a.m.–9 p.m., six days a week) work culture, besides also helping the digitally connected employees working from across different regions of China. The pressing need, for corporate China, however, was to fundamentally redefine its work environment and recognize that flexibility and autonomy needed to take root as the world moved into the *future of work*.

While China was in this time machine ahead of other countries, the trajectory followed by the rest of the world was pretty much similar. Physical offices had also long defined corporate America, even though to a lesser degree than in China. However, in a few short weeks the pandemic struck again as thousands of companies mandated that their employees work from home. In the case of corporate America, there was seemingly an early recognition of the benefits of remote working, with companies like Twitter (now X) making a public announcement as early as in May 2020 about its permanent work-from-home plans. A growing number of companies followed suit, going on to announce that they would permit employees to work remotely on a permanent basis. (It's a different matter that

X, under Elon Musk, has later changed its stance and taken a U-turn on this policy.)

Cut to two years of this work-from-home regime, however, the lessons don't seem to be enduring, as companies that once told employees that they would be working from home forever prepared to have them back at the physical office. Whether it was US President Joe Biden writing to federal workers telling them that the time was right to go back to work at their offices or the Apple chief Tim Cook outlining the company's back-to-office plan, the rhetoric was similar. JPMorgan CEO Jamie Dimon even went on to declare that remote work 'doesn't work for those who want to hustle', a clear indictment of the autonomy and agency that remote work offered, though the new world demanded them. While many companies have since brought their workers back to the office—the workers had to settle for what came to be known as 'hybrid work'—meaning, some days of the week/month at the office and other days from anywhere else. Over time, hybrid work has come to stay and is getting to be the new normal.

The story has been pretty much the same in other parts of the world too. In the UK, for example, the BBC reported that workers' search for remote roles had become more urgent, fuelled by the growing alarm that remote working opportunities might reduce in the future, what with the back-to-office rhetoric fast gaining in decibel.[5]

The India story

The India work-from-home story began with companies like Amazon, Cognizant, Flipkart, Ola Paytm, Snapdeal, Swiggy, TCS, Tech Mahindra, Uber and Wipro, which were among the first few companies to institute work-from-home policies in March 2020, when the first Covid-19 lockdown was announced. As in corporate America, in India too there were some early announcements by companies claiming to look at work from home as a long-term option.

Come end 2020, however, and it was already time for the Great Return, as the majority of workers were asked to report at their offices and trade in their sweatpants for sharp suits. This wasn't to be for too long, though, as a deadly second wave of the pandemic swept the country in 2021, forcing a return to work from home. In the see-saw that followed, the corporate world once again struggled to bring its employees back to their office desks despite the country's vaccination drive showing an upward trajectory.

A sector-wise analysis conducted by recruitment firm Randstad India in September 2022 revealed that manufacturing companies were the ones fully in favour of mandating a return to office, followed by the banking, financial services and insurance (BFSI) firms, at 68 per cent, and retail, at 57 per cent. While 53 per cent of IT and 45 per cent of business process outsourcing (BPO) companies were operating in a hybrid way, 24 per cent of BPOs and 18 per cent of IT firms were offering a work-from-home mandate.[6] More recently, another study by Indeed, the online recruitment firm, further confirmed the continued preference among companies in India for hybrid work.[7]

Hybrid work

Microsoft CEO Satya Nadella has famously referred to hybrid work as 'the biggest shift to how we work in our generation'. Whether this new hybrid structure of office work will last is, of course, unclear at this stage. If done correctly, it can certainly bring back some of the elusive balance between work and personal life that employees enjoyed during the pandemic. However, there is also the risk that office culture could degenerate into a class system, with on-site employees favoured over remote workers. The WeWork (the now bankrupt co-location space company) CEO sometime back went as far as to pronounce that the 'least engaged are very comfortable working from home', an assertion that is steeped in the centralized control-command work culture and disregards the radical reset in how people think about work and life in the post-pandemic times.

Across borders, one thing common among organizations in this regard is their lack of intention about a remote-first approach. We have seen largely tactical responses to pandemic-induced compulsions and not sustained efforts to create a robust remote work ecosystem and embrace the *future of work*. Of course, adoption of new ways of working takes significant time and change management. We need to build an operating model of work that reconciles the present differences between employers and employees on what the right balance between office-based work and other possibilities is.

That said, we see some early flickers of hope in terms of organizations recognizing that offices need to be reinvented from being places to work to places where collaboration and creativity are enabled. There have been news reports of the advertising company McCann, for example, opening new offices in the city of London, and viewing them as centres for 'creativity, collaboration and connection', in the same way that Cisco is looking at offices in the post-pandemic era as 'talent collaboration centers'.

In India too, many organizations have moved to hybrid work. Obtaining reliable and comprehensive data for India is often a challenge, but going by media reports, some of the prominent companies that have embraced hybrid work include Airtel, Hindustan Unilever (HUL), ITC, Maruti, Mercedes Benz, McCain, Mondelez, Nestlé, PepsiCo, Tech Mahindra and Swiggy.[8]

An understanding of the advantages of freeing employees from an office space had already begun to sink in among corporations, long before the pandemic. The first serious construct of remote work was formulated as 'telecommuting'. Jack Nilles, a Los Angeles-based academic, author and consultant, is said to have coined this term. Writing almost fifty years ago, in 1973, Nilles wrote in his book *The Telecommunications-Transportation Tradeoff* that telecommuting could be an 'alternative to transportation', and proposed it to be an innovative answer to the challenges of commuting and traffic congestion. Nilles said, 'Technology was not the limiting factor in the acceptance of telecommuting.' Instead, he said, 'organizational—and management—cultural changes were far more important in the rate of acceptance of telecommuting'.[9] So true even today, after fifty years!

A lot has been written about telecommuting since, providing many insights around its implications for work, workers, managers and the environment. A credible contemporary voice delineating the *future of work* is that of Nicholas Bloom, a professor in the department of economics at Stanford University. In his 2017 TEDx Stanford talk, he referred to work from home as 'a future-looking technology'. This was his conclusion after his conduct of a large-scale experiment that proved the efficacy of remote work without a doubt. In his graduate economics class, he narrated a story about James Liang, co-founder and CEO of Ctrip, China's largest travel agency, which had a workforce of 16,000. 'One day while James and I were talking, he mentioned Ctrip was interested in allowing its Shanghai employees to work from home,' Bloom said. However, without hard data, the company was reluctant to make dramatic changes in its telecommuting policy.

Bloom and Liang ran a randomized controlled trial in which over 500 employees of the call centre at the travel agency volunteered to participate. One of the important qualifications for employees to work from home was to have a private room to themselves and decent broadband access. While some of these people were selected to telecommute four days of the week, others remained in the office as a control group.

When they reviewed the results, Ctrip had saved $1900 per employee over the course of the study—which was expected. More importantly, the remote employees were 13.5 per cent more productive than the employees who worked out of office. The people working from home also reported taking shorter breaks, fewer sick days and less time off. Also, the attrition rates among the at-home group were 50 per cent lower than among the office group. Most importantly, the remote employees reported significantly higher job satisfaction levels.[10]

Another seminal piece of research, undertaken by Prithwiraj Choudhury, an associate professor at Harvard Business School, was about a work-from-anywhere scheme that had started in 2012 at the United States Patent & Trademark Office (USPTO). The study concluded that the arrangement had boosted productivity by 4.4 per cent, as measured by the number of patent applications examined each month. Participating employees reported that work flexibility had also improved the quality of their lives.[11]

Prithwiraj also points to findings from a 2020 field experiment that he and his colleagues from Harvard Business School and Stanford University ran on hybrid working with 130-odd members of the admin staff at the Bangladesh Rural Advancement Committee, a large NGO. They found that over a nine-week period, employees who spent between 23 per cent and 40 per cent of their working time in the office had found the optimum combination, a sweet spot of sorts, where they enjoyed flexibility and yet didn't get a feeling of isolation while at work. It was the people in this group that produced original work, as also received better performance ratings.[12] According to Bloom, people value hybrid work at somewhere between 7 per cent and 8 per cent of pay increase, and the format is here to stay as people increasingly put a premium on work-life balance.[13]

My own learnings from a doctoral dissertation that I guided and supervised in India presented some key insights on the impact of remote work. This study used linear regression analysis on survey data collected from a sample of 446 professionals working with a software company in the city of Hyderabad, India. The analysis revealed no direct negative effect of remote work arrangements on employee engagement and performance.[14]

Little surprise, then, that since the Covid-19 pandemic we have seen some very irreversible preferences for hybrid work models emerge. During the forced lockdowns, employees realized two things: that they inherently wanted the flexibility and freedom to choose when to work, and from where; and that home or other non-office locations were good and viable alternatives to the office. People also realized that they were not going to office only to work, and that in fact the office was more a place for socializing. As the world opened up after the pandemic, the understanding was that while people wanted the comfort and bonhomie of the office, which two centuries of office going had got them used to, they didn't want to be bound by it.

It is this same priority—of providing work flexibility—that has also led to a four-day workweek pilot in recent times. In 2019, Microsoft Japan tested a four-day work week, where work hours decreased overall. Staff productivity showed a nearly 40 per cent increase.

Researchers at the Independent London-based think tank Autonomy along with two non-profits—4 Day Week Global and 4 Day Week UK Campaign—conducted a six-month study on the impact of a four-day work-week across sixty-one companies in the UK. Their study found that 15 per cent of employees who participated in the study said 'no amount of money' would convince them to go back to working five days a week. The trial was the latest to validate the need to adopt more flexible work practices.[15]

The march towards flexibility gained momentum post our experience with Covid-19 pandemic. This epoch-making event will stand out for bringing several fundamental shifts in how we work, how we design organizations and how we lead people. I would highlight five significant after-effects of the pandemic which should inform our thinking about what we should do in the matter of work post-Covid.

The 5 Ds accentuated by the Covid-19 pandemic

Digitalization: Clearly, the Covid-19 pandemic exponentially accelerated adoption of digitalization across sectors all over the world. The first obvious change triggered by the large-scale adoption of digitalization is that organizations can now be 'platforms' transacting almost everything on the Internet. Old formats such as hierarchies, departments, cabins and other brick-and-mortar structures are increasingly being rendered redundant. The digitally enabled distributed organization of the future will demand a distributed leadership model.

Decentralization: There is a definite breakdown of single-source supply chains. The gigantic and concentrated supply behemoths of the business world are now required to create more hub-and-spoke models. What this also implies is adaption to a more agile, bottom-up and fluid organizational design. In this context, we must refer to the unconventional organizational model that the Chinese company Haier (a global home appliances and consumer electronics company) has been following. As its CEO Zhang Ruimin says: 'Since the industrial revolution more than 100 years ago, the American model—a bureaucratic model—has prevailed. What we want to do is to overthrow the old models . . .' After it eliminated the bureaucracy, the organization was no longer hierarchical. It became a decentralized, distributed network. Haier has abolished over 12,000 middle-manager jobs and created 'microenterprises', where self-managed teams connect with customers directly, without any intermediation. Such decentralized arrangements will be the future of organizational design.

Devolution: The pandemic has proven the prudence of devolution of decision-making and empowerment of the grassroots people in no uncertain terms. Consider the project for the setting up of oxygen plants across states and union territories in India. Funded by the government, and with regional and private-sector backing, oxygen plants can now be set up at the local level. India has finally passed on the authority for this to the grassroots level after the debacle of oxygen shortage in the country during the second wave of the pandemic.

Getting back to workplaces, in particular, the pandemic has been a huge eye-opener when it comes to the ineffectuality of the centralized command-control cultures of decision-making, drawing our attention back to the time-honoured wisdom of self-management. It has taken people several decades to realize that the military model of the office, as we know it, is broken. In the post-pandemic world, leaders will be best served to empower the frontline and bottom-of-the-pyramid employees by devolving more powers to them.

Democratization: While civilizational progress has always meant a greater voice for the people, sometimes it takes a crisis (read: a pandemic) to reinforce and advance this belief. The mighty Chinese government had to recently rescind its zero-Covid strategy following protests by its people, reaffirming how people want to have a say on issues that matter to them. Similarly, India saw its farm laws being repealed after massive demonstrations against them. Just as ordinary citizens demand a greater say in matters concerning their lives, so do employees want a greater say in matters concerning their companies. Going forward, social media will only accelerate these democratic choices. Organizations can only choose to disregard employee voices at their own peril.

Disruption (not merely change) marks the world of today. The Covid-19 pandemic is the best example from which to understand how volatility, uncertainty, complexity and ambiguity come together at certain times, disrupting everything all at once.

It is really this big picture of the pandemic that needs to inform our understanding of what needs to be done with work formats and organizations at large. The debate on the *future of work,* therefore, needs to be framed and appreciated against this massive canvas. Seen this way, the debate as to whether employees should work from office or home may seem inconsequential, as would be the tactical power struggle on who decides when employees should come to office. Instead, we need to ask the larger question: How we can anticipate, grasp, embrace and deal with the transition from command, control and regimentation to self-determination, autonomy and flexibility, the three key imperatives accelerated by the Covid-19 pandemic?

New business models in the post-pandemic era will compel leaders to constantly up-skill their employees. Not just the pandemic, future disruptions such as climate change will require companies to build resilient capabilities to renew and upgrade the skills of their employees on an on-going basis

While we may have lost several lives to the coronavirus, it will be a shame to waste this crisis and not learn from it. Taking advantage of the paradigm shifts that Covid-19 has triggered, we particularly need to revisit our conventional approaches to the three urgent requirements in India—creation of sufficient formalized employment, living-wage jobs and sustainable skills. This calls us to shape and steer the *future of work* to address the country's unique socio-economic needs.

Flexibility: The new currency of work

Both the immediate needs of India and the emerging global trends in work and employment can be addressed if we go beyond the binary debate of office or home. We should see this era as marking the final assertion of 'flexibility' as the new currency in the world of work. Given the long colonial and feudal history of India, its managers and leaders will take longer to embrace flexibility in the country's evolution into a forward-looking society. For decades, we have seen flexibility as the privilege of a few, while the majority must submit to meaningless regimentation. This practice is reinforced by an underlying mindset of presenteeism, which equates physical presence with productivity.

I believe that overcoming this limiting mindset will be in our societal and national interest. We must embrace flexibility, especially in work and employment models, to be able to connect Bharat (the vast majority of rural and semi-urban India) with India and its more visible urban centres like Mumbai, Delhi, Bengaluru, etc. We must appreciate that the pandemic and many other forces of the present times have started shaping a whole new work order underpinned by flexibility.

A more detailed discussion of the emerging global discourse on the *future of work* will put things in perspective. As we will see in the next chapter, the exciting new possibilities around the intersection between technology, people and societies will tell us more about the rewards and risks the *future of work* holds for us.

3

Future of Work

The Global Discourse and the India Perspective

The 'future of work' depends very much on where you are in the world. Most discussions in the West focus on how technological evolution in the West affects jobs in the West. This frame is too narrow for the twenty-first century: we must investigate the effect of technological change on work everywhere.

—Robert C. Allen[1]

Apart from 'flexibility' as the new currency of the world of work, there are several other urgent issues that the emergent global discourse on the *future of work* deals with. Separately, while scanning the global discussions on the topic, we must also analyse how India needs to embrace global learning and rapidly adopt the advances in new tech-enabled employment models. While being informed by the global discourse on the *future of work*, India must shape its own trajectory and address some of its unique challenges, especially in generating inclusive quality employment opportunities for millions on a large scale.

Tracing the history of the *future of work*, as it were, one is sure to be led to John Maynard Keynes's seminal essay, 'The Economic Possibilities for our Grandchildren', written as early as in 1930.

'What can we reasonably expect the level of our economic life to be a hundred years hence? What are the economic possibilities for our grandchildren?' Keynes asked in that essay. The answer, according to him, lay in the fact that human needs 'fall into two classes'—needs that are absolute, and needs that are relative (those whose satisfaction makes us feel superior to others). He reasoned that while the needs of the second class may be insatiable, the absolute needs will soon be satisfied. Having concluded that *economic problems* may be solved, or at least be within sight of solution, Keynes envisaged 'three-hour shifts or a fifteen-hour week' becoming the order of the day within a hundred years. The real issue in Keynes's analysis was that in the face of satisfaction of these economic needs, man would 'be faced with his real, his permanent problem – how to use his freedom from pressing economic cares, how to occupy the leisure, which science and compound interest will have won for him, to live wisely and agreeably and well'; especially since as a race 'we have been trained too long to strive and not to enjoy'.[2]

As we head to the 100-year mark of Keynes's prophecy, we are beginning to see economic prosperity, short working hours and a good balanced life in certain parts of the world. Some of the Nordic countries inspire us in this respect, by consistently turning up at the top of the happiness index.

As we speculate on how to shape the *future of work*, it is debatable if work itself will have a future, considering the developments described above. But that is a different topic of discussion, and many at the present stage of development in India might find this too futuristic

However, as the futurist Paul Saffo has said, thinking about the future is 'what defines us as a species'.[3] In keeping with that tradition, let us look at how work will change in the medium term. Some of the top themes that describe the contemporary discourse on the *future of work* include:

Automation and robotization; implications for jobs and employment

Ever since the Industrial Revolution, there have been concerns around machines pushing up productivity on the one hand but making human labour obsolete on the other. So much so that the stocking-frame operators of Nottingham in the UK wrecked improved knitting machines in the 1760s, which they saw as a threat to their jobs. Remember the famous Luddite movement in the early nineteenth century?[4] With AI and robots slated to replace millions of jobs, there is a lot of debate around the efficiency that they will bring on the one hand and the job losses they will cause on the other. The stock answer, of course, is that technological progress will aid development at large, and just as technological progress in the past three centuries led to increasing incomes, it will continue to do so in the future too.

Forecasts, such as those of the World Economic Forum's on the *future of work,* show that many jobs will be disrupted but that sizeable numbers of new job roles will emerge too. The net effect would be an increase in jobs. WEF estimates that while 85 million jobs will go by 2025, 97 million new roles will emerge in the same period.[5]

An MIT report on the future of work also argues that fears about job displacement due to AI are overblown. The report predicts that AI will create more jobs than it will destroy.

On the other hand, many economic theorists also sound a word of caution. Robert C. Allen, professor of economic history at New York University Abu Dhabi, for example, reminds us that the past shouldn't be held as a blueprint for the future. What worked in the past is what Allen calls 'feedback loops between education and technology'. He explains how:

> . . . rising incomes led to the demand for fancier manufactured goods; markets, therefore, encouraged technological change and led to jobs that were performed more effectively by educated people. The increasing number of educated people, in turn, prompted the invention of technologies that took advantage of education. It thus led to a self-fulfilling cycle. At the same time, the state helped spread the benefits of this economic development across the population.[6]

He believes that the loop between education and technology may not kick in as efficiently as before, and therefore the lost manufacturing jobs on account of technology may not be more than made up by knowledge-based jobs.

At this point we can only make educated guesses about job disruption and the resulting balance that will emerge. In my view, while over time (say over ten to fifteen years) the balance may reset, a generation or even more will lose jobs and their skills will be rendered obsolete, widening income and employment gaps, especially in countries like India. Further, societies will be faced with a massive reskilling/upskilling burden, making the task of generating employment for all very onerous. India must learn from Europe. The European Commission is proactively convening the European Employment & Social Rights Forum 2023 on how AI is shaping work. We in India must ask the same questions: How do we make AI at work fair for everyone? How do we ensure AI-driven work is equal and transparent? How safe will AI-led *future of work* be for India's vastly unequal society?

Rapid skills obsolescence, reskilling and upskilling

As we stand at the beginning of the fourth Industrial Revolution, the lines between the physical, digital and biological spheres are blurring. There is a gap between the skills needed for the fourth Industrial Revolution and the skills current employees have. WEF estimates that one quarter of the technologically displaced workforce in the US could be successfully reskilled at an investment of $4.7 billion, with a positive cost-benefit balance.[7] It is a given that people will need to get on the treadmill of learning. While the personal agency of workers to do that is a prerequisite, that alone isn't enough. As Lynda Gratton, professor at London Business School points out, corporations will need to step up and help create new pools of talent in each local community. The very technologies that can render many unskilled and unemployable can be leveraged to up-skill them. Needless to mention, there will be an increasing need for government-supported activities as the cost of reskilling and upskilling themselves on their own will be an unfair burden on the people, to say the least.

Human–machine cohabitation and interfaces

With the ubiquitous use of new-age machines and robots, far-reaching changes in the socio-emotional lives of humans will be triggered. To share work and cohabit with intelligent robots will be arduous for humans. As technology becomes intelligent, screen-less, seamless and sensing, humans will need to learn how to coexist, build trust in and work alongside machines.

Remote and hybrid work

That technological advances are enabling work from just about anywhere is a given. Additionally, there is the impact of millennials and Gen-Z employees entering the workforce, about which much has been written. Younger employees want work to be flexible and to integrate with their lifestyles. They prefer to work from wherever they are most comfortable and productive and expect employers to support their evolving work preferences. The rise of 'pub desks', for example, stands testimony to the fact that work need not be confined to the four walls of the office any more.

What is more, several studies are suggesting that hybrid work does not adversely affect productivity or worker satisfaction.[8] While remote work is a growing discipline for the individual worker, it is distributed work that will be a discipline for the entire organization. The *future of work* enables seamless integration of people spread across geographies, including in traditional office spaces and remote locations, which could mean home offices, co-working spaces, workcations and every location from where digital nomads work on the go.

Organizational redesign and rethinking people management

Other than a distributed workforce, what is also likely to emerge is a structural overhaul, a potent redesign of organizational models themselves. We may have to change how we design organizations and respond to people's unique needs.[9] 'Networks', as opposed to traditional 'hierarchies', will be the new organizational form. Further, there will grow an agile workforce that will adapt to new ways of working and new job requirements.

As organizations try to be agile to combat the pressures of an ever-changing environment, and with workers preferring flexibility, workforce composition may have to be significantly reimagined. Organizations will increasingly use independent workers, freelancers, gig or crowd-sourced workers. Firms will increasingly fill critical skill gaps with interim high-skilled workers, such as AI/ML experts, agile coaches or blockchain experts, instead of hiring full-time employees.

The demands of the *future of work*, therefore, require that organizations make changes to their talent management strategies. Blending and balancing different types of workers—not all full time—will be the new name of the game.

Social changes in attitudes towards work, combined with the freedom that technology brings people, will challenge traditional management practices head-on. Managerial authority reinforced by command-control organizations will soon be a thing of the past. Organizations that do not embrace flexibility and autonomy as prerequisites for performance and engagement will lose the race to attract and retain talent.

Work and life: Balance, integration and fit

The separation of work and personal life, as we know, is changing. The *future of work,* particularly, will make it difficult to maintain water-tight compartments between work and life. The new generation of workforce does not appreciate the conventional boundaries between home and work. They hate to be confined to a desk to get work done. They are questioning the long hours, the hustle culture and the rationale of 'presenteeism' of the previous generations. As they value their personal freedom, they expect to be given some discretion when it comes to choosing their place of work and the time in their lives that this work will take.

With knowledge emerging as the most valuable capital, innovation and creativity are at a premium. Clearly, then, the old-world order of placing people in a confined space for a fixed number of hours with people watching over them, for good measure, will not work. The *future of work* will witness reconsideration of the conventional ways of working as well as reconciliation to the fact that the number of hours spent at work does not necessarily correlate with productivity.

Considering the above, work-life balance is slated to acquire a whole different perspective. 'The five-day week is not the ultimate, and neither is the eight-hour day,' Henry Ford had said as early as in 1926.[10] Going forward, work-life balance will have a lot to do with freedom and flexibility. Workers will increasingly demand more flexibility and more choice in deciding when, where and how to best do their jobs. And progressive employers will begin many new experiments with work flexibility.

Another dimension of flexibility would be the guaranteeing of employees' free time after their work hours. Portugal recently introduced a law banning employers from contacting workers outside of their regular hours by phone, messaging or email.

A common thread in all these developments is not so much the movement towards reduced work hours but the reassertion of 'flexibility' as the new normal in the world of work.

Governance models for AI/ML use and data protection

The coming together of powerful data analytics and global information platforms, along with the changing social attitudes towards personal data, is likely to give rise to several privacy challenges. The *future of work* in such a scenario demands a policy-informed technical approach to these challenges. What is important is to lead a global dialogue with policymakers, civil society and industry leaders to shape the future of privacy and data governance. Initiatives such as the MIT Future of Data—a lab initiative with the goal of bringing state-of-the-art computer science research together with world-leading public policy expertise and engagement—are steps in the right direction. No wonder that many governments are increasingly concerned about governing AI. The United Kingdom hosted the first international AI Safety Summit in November 2023 to discuss and agree on the urgent need to govern AI developments. The United States government issued an executive order on safe, secure and trustworthy artificial intelligence in 2023 to address the growing concerns over the use of AI. Though yet to firm up specific measures, India too has started work in this area. As early as in 2018, India put together its initial thoughts on it in its 'National Artificial Intelligence Strategy'. It formulated 'Principles for Responsible AI' in 2021.[11]

Social and employment security

While governments are focused on data privacy and prevention of abuse of AI, the bigger problem is loss of jobs and widening income inequality. Evidently prosperous nations too have glaring income disparities. The United States, for example, has substantially higher income disparity than any other developed nation, and this is rising, with the incomes of the highest echelon of earners rapidly outpacing that of the rest of the population. Even among high earners, income gains have been heavily skewed towards the top of that bracket. The well-known Gini index must remind us of the acute nature of this problem.[12] It's apt here to remember what the United Nations special rapporteur on extreme poverty and human rights, Philip Alston, said: 'The American Dream is rapidly becoming the American illusion, as the US now has the lowest rate of social mobility of any of the rich countries.'[13]

It stands to reason, then, that if machines are introduced in the interest of efficiency, what needs added focus is protection of people from the ensuing 'technological unemployment' and further rise in inequities. In short, what needs to be protected is universal basic income (UBI). UBI is an old idea that has had support from conservatives like Milton Friedman and progressives such as Martin Luther King Jr alike. In fact, a lot of interest in UBI has been rekindled by Silicon Valley, with tech giants being concerned about AI replacing humans in the workforce. Some form of UBI, by way of the MNREGA scheme, exists in India, which gives a legal guarantee of 100 days of wage employment in a financial year to adult members of a rural household who demand employment and volunteer to do unskilled manual work. However, MGNREGA is still a bridge between traditional employment and unemployment. The need of the hour is to go beyond it as technology gains pace.

The Indian perspective

India is currently consuming Western narratives on the future of work. We are yet to evolve our own. Professors Schlogl, Weiss and Prainsack at the University of Vienna explain with convincing data how discourse on the future of work is dominated by the West.[14] Here is the summary of their study of 195 documents published in English (2013–2018) to understand what problem perceptions, frames and policy recommendations prevail in the literature on the *Future of Work:*

- Most *future of work* narratives emerge mainly from the global North/advanced West (>80% from North America and Europe).
- 25 per cent of all major reports are by consulting companies.
- These treat the *future of work* as a problem emerging only from technological advances.
- Most of these studies assume that technology must dictate the structure, content and requirements of work.

- People are called upon to adapt. But upskilling jobseekers without job creation is flawed, as was pointed out by the late Alice Amsden, noted professor and development economist at MIT.[15]
- The *future of work* has been painted predominantly as technological determinism.
- All the analyses conceptually close the door to manifold pathways or possibilities of work.
- Most of these studies are largely led by business consulting groups who have a vested interest in framing the problem in a way that offers business consultancy opportunities to them in reconfiguring the workforce as an automatic solution.

These findings compel us to build an alternative Indian perspective on the *future of work* by factoring in India's own unique socio-economic considerations. Here are a few to consider:

The changing and multi-tiered rural–urban landscape

Popular reportage often speaks of two Indias—the shining urban India and its poorer cousin, Bharat. While this scenario is fast changing, the fact remains that India comprises a multi-tiered rural-urban landscape. While India's small towns are extremely aspirational, they are in acute need of formal and well-paid jobs. Not only will robust job availability improve the ecosystem of towns and cities, but it will also reduce the load of migration on the larger cities, which are already bursting at the seams. In shaping the *future of work,* India needs to therefore look at its own unique characteristics, which we will discuss in some detail in a later chapter. In this context, a recent report on 'emerging technology hubs of India' by Nasscom and Deloitte provides us with rich data and insights on the potential of a large number of two-tier cities, like Ranchi, Raipur, Hubbali, Nashik, Vellore, Guwahati, Tiruchirappally, etc. Already, up to 15 per cent of the country's talent resides in these 'second wave' towns. Smaller towns produce 60 per cent of the graduates in India. Beyond these second-wave towns, there could be another 200+ towns that can grow to be the face of new India—if invested in and built carefully.

Women's participation in work

Conventional wisdom suggests that in a growing economy, as education levels rise, more women will enter the paid workforce. India's experience, however, is the contrary. While India's population is growing, women's participation in its workforce is shrinking. The World Bank figures say that women represented 23 per cent of India's formal and informal workforce in 2021, down from nearly 27 per cent in 2005. While India is aiming to be a $5-trillion economy, it must leverage women's talent, especially the capabilities of its rural women, who must become part of the growing human capital pool. In fact, the challenge for India is not merely to increase participation by women in the labour force but to draw up the policies and investments required to provide 'quality' jobs to women.

In this context, I must refer to two important government initiatives: 1. Deen Dayal Upadhyaya Grameen Kaushalya Yojana (DDU-GKY)[16] and 2. Pradhan Mantri Gramin Digital Saksharta Abhiyan.(PMGDISHA)[17] DDU-GKY aims to skill rural youth who are poor and provide them with jobs having regular monthly wages or above the minimum wages. PMGDISHA is a central government scheme to empower rural youth to be digitally literate. These must be properly executed to bridge the rural–urban divide. Large-scale skilling of women must be taken up. Ensuring equal access to mobile phones and broadband Internet will reduce gender gaps in these areas.

The joint family system

If there is one cementing force at the heart of traditional Indian society, it is our joint family system—an institution by itself and a typical symbol of the collectivist culture of India. While this social construct, at first glance, may seem like it has nothing to do with the *future of work*, the fact remains that economic policies and work policies should aim to protect this institution, as opposed to destroying it. The availability of remote jobs, especially in small towns and villages, can be a big step in this direction. Well-thought-through, joint-family-friendly employment models and policies can prevent unnecessary migration and minimize the break-up of joint family systems, which are vital to the continuation of India's unique social protection system.

Stark socio-economic inequities

We have already addressed the need to design *future of work* policies taking into account the existing socio-economic inequities, as also the ones that the technological revolution is likely to perpetuate. In the context of India, its importance cannot be overstated. The top 10 per cent of the Indian population holds 77 per cent of the total national wealth.[18] It is particularly alarming that Indian society is fractured along the lines of caste and religion. Growing economic inequities will only exacerbate these issues. The need for governmental systems to step up and offer support in creating easy-to-access, flexible employment opportunities with decent wages cannot be emphasized enough.

Millennials and the rising aspirations of youth

With over 600 million people between the ages of eighteen and thirty-five, India has the largest number of millennials and the Gen Z globally. Look at the implications: 37 per cent of millennials are likely to switch employers in the next twelve months. While employers have so far been more focused on building a resilient workforce strategy, employees, on their part, are driven by opportunities for fulfilment, creativity, innovation and authenticity, apart from financial rewards, says PwC's India Workforce Hopes and Fears Survey 2022.[19]

The *future of work* policies in India must be tailored to meet the needs and aspirations of the MZ generation (millennials + Gen Z). All organizations, large or small, must shift their focus from loyalty, seniority, long-term careers, etc., to learning, growth and flexibility (hybrid work), and foster a culture of trust, empathy, open communication, collaboration and co-creation.

Colonial hangover and status/privilege orientation

Whether or not we admit it, there is a strong status/privilege orientation in India, a result perhaps of our colonial and feudal past. The resistance to give up command-

and-control managerial styles, especially among older employees, is our unique problem. Technology is a leveller. On a Zoom call, everyone is an icon side by side. The deep desire to boss over others and entrench a class system in the workplace is incompatible with the egalitarianism that modern technology-led workplaces can offer. It will be easier for Indians to adopt the trappings of technology than to work without the privileges of the corner office and the power of having people at their beck and call. My guess as to why the big bosses in India resist virtual video call-based work is that they don't like the idea of 'scheduling' a meeting with lower-level employees. All these years they just had them show up whenever they wanted them to, for they had them captive in cubicles right under their nose. Now they must request them in advance for a meeting and send them an invite. This is loss of power. (Remember, telling someone '*Sahab yaad kar rahe hain*', literally, 'the boss is remembering you', has been for decades office euphemism to tell someone that the boss wants him in his office.)

These tendencies won't go away overnight. Culture is hard to change. All this is just to say that the *future of work* in India will have to contend with the terrible past of bossism and class divide at the workplace. This would not be the case in some of the Western countries that have managed to build more egalitarian societies.

The course of the *future of work* must be suitably modified and adjusted to India's unique needs. We may minimize and be more circumspect about the job-eliminating technologies around AI/ML, and yet we may embrace the power of remote, asynchronous, video-based work, for it will suit our millennials to stay in their villages and get to do decent jobs. Overall, whatever we do will demand extraordinary flexibility on the part of employers, governments and the workforce itself.

4

The Rise of the Remote and Flexible Work Order

It's okay if newspapers get it wrong, as long as the history books get it right.

—Sam Altman[1]

People had always wanted flexibility at work. And the twin forces of digital technologies and the Covid-19 pandemic showed us that rigidities around time and place of work are not mandatory for productive work. But our pandemic-induced work arrangements, at best, have been rather tactical and emergency responses to a health crisis. Whether our choosing to work from home or, later, after missing the socialization at the office, our return to the workplace in some measure (hybrid work)—both are afterthoughts and coping mechanisms. As we wrestle with the post-pandemic world and experience new crises due to climate change, we will refine our choices about how and where to work. Further, as access to far more seamless and immersive video and digitally enabled work tools becomes possible, more flexible options around work will emerge. The big picture is clear: future work arrangements will be underpinned by 'flexibility' and 'virtual' work.

Flexibility will inform the new work order at three levels: i) Individual preferences for work models and arrangements, ii) Team arrangements for collective work, and iii) Organizational coping, with the new demands for flexibility in terms of employment models as well as workspace design.

Several different surveys in recent years have been suggesting a clear preference for flexibility among millennials.[2]

The statistics are similar the world over. Clearly, flexibility as to place, time and modes of work is what an entire generation of workers across borders are asking for.

For employers, flexibility translates into widening the pool of talent, retention of staff, bridging of critical skill gaps and a lot more. Importantly, as a Gallup study noted, flexible work also drives employee engagement, which in turn results in enhanced productivity, including but not limited to lower absenteeism and higher profitability[3]. The demand for flexibility has been further enhanced by the growth of automation and AI. Capgemini's Fluid Workforce Research says that as much as 71 per cent of organizations rely on fluid workers because of the ever-changing skill requirements presented by AI and automation. Further, more than 60 per cent of organizations agree that AI and automation have created new job roles that are undertaken by fluid workers.[4]

While we tend to speak of the rise of a flexible work order in the post-pandemic world with broad brush strokes, what we are referring to are at least two broad facets of it:

I. How flexible work is tactically contracted and delivered, both from the individual as well as organizational point of view.
II. How organizations need to be strategically redesigned to accommodate this flexibility.

It will be worth looking at both these aspects in some detail.

Contracting and delivering work

The new changes to how work is contracted and delivered are best described by the emerging expression 'fluid workforce'. This new work format is characterized by personalized working hours, the employees' ability to choose to operate from anywhere in the world, and their defying of traditional hierarchical structures.

To put this in context, we must refer to Zygmunt Bauman, a Polish sociologist, who coined the terms 'liquid modernity' and 'liquid society'. Applied to employees, they signify a workforce that avoids stagnation or unjustified stability and flows instead, on account of its distinctive liquidity. These concepts break several decades of tradition, where organizations had come to rely on full-time employees alone, with tightly defined roles and skill sets.[5]

Importantly, what liquid work allows corporations to do is to find professionals not only with highly specialized skill sets but who also work in a distributed manner to deliver at speed. What it offers is an 'agile' workforce, contracted differently—as full-time employees, as professionals working on output-based contracts, as virtual teams and in many other different forms.

In terms of the individual, flexible work can take many forms, covering the axes of both place and time. Formal full-time employees can move from being place-constrained (read: work from the office) to place-unconstrained (read: work from anywhere); as also from being time-constrained (working 9–5, working synchronously with others) to being time-unconstrained (working asynchronously).[6] Simply put, with the advent of flexible work, work is no longer restricted to a time and a place but is an activity you can undertake any time and anywhere.

In addition, flexible working, from the individual point of view, can take the form of part-time work, compressed hours, flexi-time and job-shares, freelance work, gig work, contracting and portfolio careers, paid crowd work, moonlighting and more.

Interestingly, this flexibility is not only taking shape by way of organizational policies but also by way of countrywide legislation. A new human resource law in the UAE, for example, aims to develop a flexible working model to manage human resources as well as to improve government efficiencies.[7] The five work patterns outlined in the human resources law in the UAE are:

- **Work from the office:** Employees are required to come to the main office or a branch during official working hours.
- **Work remotely (within the UAE):** Employees may work from anywhere provided they are working from within the UAE.
- **Work remotely (from outside the UAE):** Employees are also allowed work from outside the country.
- **Shorter work week** (compressed working hours): Employees may choose to work for lesser number of days in a week (like 4 days) by opting to work for longer hours everyday.

- **Hybrid work:** This model allows employees to work out of their homes a few days of the week and the other days from office, as mutually agreed upon with the employer.

As flexibility becomes integral to the contemporary workplace, what is equally important is adoption of a long-term holistic view of the employee company's offerings, in which flexibility isn't the sole ingredient. It stands to reason that greater flexibility at work requires organizational redesign, a change in working methodologies as well as new leadership styles based on a decentralized ethos, which at its core calls for trust in teams. It stands to reason, then, that incorporation of flexibility at the workplace requires going beyond making small tweaks to human resource policies and reimagining the entire organization as well as resetting relationships.

Human-centric flexible organizations

The key question is, where can companies start? While remote work, a four-day work week or hybrid work may be the most popular flexibility options for employees, none of them is a panacea. What matters is enhancement of organizational capability to handle the concept of flexible work.

In their book *Humanocracy, Creating Organisations as Amazing as the People Inside Them*, Gary Hamel and Michel Zanini make a strong case for 'humanocracy' and for 'poking the bureaucratic beehive'.

'Our organizations are failing us,' they point out. 'They're sluggish, change-phobic and emotionally arid. Human beings, by contrast, are adaptable, creative and full of passion.' The gap between individual and organizational capability, as they point out, 'is the unfortunate by-product of bureaucracy; the top-down, rule-choked management structure that undergirds virtually every organization on the planet'. They go on to add that bureaucracy was 'invented in the nineteenth century with the goal of turning people into semi-programmable robots', and that it is 'deeply dehumanizing'. [8]

However, the good news, the authors reveal, is that 'there are compelling, workable alternatives to the organizational status quo and a way to get from here to there—though it'll take some bushwhacking'. Some of the elements of the DNA of a human-centric organization include: prioritization of principles over practices, ownership, meritocracy, openness and experimentation.

This is not a can-be-done but a must-do shift, as the stakes are high and workforce redesign impacts attraction, retention and innovation.

Several redesign frameworks have been suggested by organization design specialists. One practical framework for redesigning the organizational model[9] looks at two elements—work interdependence and work autonomy— and evaluation of the workforce based on the extent to which the organization depends on interactions with external labour and the degree of freedom employees are given to decide how their work is done.

Importantly, redesigning work is more about the humans involved as opposed to the tasks involved. It is when a system of working acknowledges the capabilities and motivations of its workers that you will have a happy and productive workforce. This approach also involves taking traditional managerial practices head on and replacing the conventional command-control approaches of leadership with curious inquiry. Peter Drucker once said, 'The leader of the past knew how to tell. The leader of the future will know how to ask.' While command-and-control leaders insist on discipline, structure and hierarchy in designing organizations, leaders of the future will shape them more as networks of self-managed teams.

In this context, it is worth noting the unconventional model of Haier, the well-known Chinese home appliances company. Zhang Ruimin, Haier's famous CEO, in an interview with *McKinsey Quarterly*, says: 'In our *Rendanheyi* model, the value of each individual is reflected in the value they create for users. Establishing our model disrupts everything traditional, such as hierarchy and bureaucracy, because everyone has direct contact with the users, the end consumers.'[10]

Such models will surely inspire future organizations. However, it is important is that flexibility does not degenerate into some fancy employer-brand initiative. Embrace of true flexibility involves more than just having some online tool kits or self-scheduling software or even just compiling a scrum team. So far, leaders have been managing flexibility tactically, seen often as accommodation around individual life events. Even where flexibility is adopted a little more seriously, it tends to pass on the buck to the workers, creating two classes of flexibility, with the top leaders rewarding themselves with flexible schedules as entitlement and grudgingly offering them to frontline workers and sometimes penalizing them for it. Research done by Ernst & Young indicates that about one in six workers has even suffered some negative consequences, such as poorer pay or loss of promotion opportunities because of a flexible work schedule, in what is known as 'flexibility stigma' at work.[11]

True flexibility is possible only when there is equal opportunity for both workers and managers to avail of flexibility—which is not seen as a privilege for some but as a necessary condition for productive and engaged work for all. This will require that the necessary scaffolding is provided through organizational beliefs, commitments and policies. Importantly, all of this requires a resetting of the organizational culture based on trust. As we bring in a diverse set of employees with different needs, like formal full-time employees, independent contractors, telecommuters, gig workers, etc., one-size-fits-all organizational policies won't work.

Multiple benefits of flexibility

Many studies since the 1990s have reported positive associations between flexible and/or alternative work arrangements—like compressed work weeks—and many individual and organizational outcomes like productivity, satisfaction, absenteeism, etc.[12] Let's look at two specific studies that suggest how the overall attractiveness of organizations goes up as a result of flexibility and how health outcomes among employees improve:

Employee health

One meta-analytic review examined the relationship between flexible work arrangements and health behaviours and outcomes. It found that flexible work arrangements are positively associated with better physical health, reduced absenteeism and fewer somatic symptoms—all suggesting that flexible work arrangements can facilitate employees in maintaining their health.[13]

Organizational attractiveness

Meta-analytic results based on sixty-eight studies and 52,738 employees indicate that flexible work practices increase organizational attractiveness. Of course, the extent of this attractiveness depends on how people anticipate organizational support.[14]

Small companies are adopting flexibility

In the United States, a leading study recently found that 76 per cent of companies with under 500 employees now offer full work-location flexibility or have gone fully remote.[15] Since India often follows the corporate practices of the US, our small firms too will be well advised to adopt this useful practice and benefit from the huge cost savings and enhanced employee morale that will result. By the way, it is not only tech companies—56 per cent of non-tech companies too are adopting flexible work practices in the US.[16]

Dr Gleb Tsipursky, lauded as office whisperer and hybrid expert by the *New York Times*, boldly asserts: 'And the flexible work revolution is just getting started. As the next generations of firms grow they will force change at the dinosaurs clinging to rigid in-office traditions.'[17]

As we conclude this chapter, it is important to ask, one more time, if all this flexibility applies only to white-collar employees. Contrary to this popular belief, flexibility is not the privilege of the white-collar workforce only. Blue-collar workers toiling in factories and other workers slogging in farms, stores and warehouses can avail themselves of flexible work arrangements. We will attempt to bust this and some other myths around work flexibility in the next chapter.

5

Are Flexible Work Options Only for IT and White-Collar Workforces?

Seeing is NOT believing. Believing is seeing.[1]

As we saw in the last chapter, a flexible work order is gradually getting mainstreamed into the world of work. Flexibility around time and place of work, as well as a new flexible work ethos that sheds the rigidities in work structure, work design, hiring considerations, etc., are now increasingly being adopted by progressive employers. However, the option to work remotely from home or any non-office location continues to be the most important indicator of flexibility at the workplace. IT companies have largely embraced the remote or hybrid work choice, and it is they who come to mind whenever we think of flexible work. In this chapter, we will examine how flexible work options and, particularly, remote work options are not limited to IT companies.

Think of remote work and you almost always imagine an IT geek in casual tees sitting down to code at leisure.

Let your imagination run a little wild, and you tend to build a picture of another knowledge worker taking a 'workcation', sitting on an idyllic beach with a pitcher of beer and a laptop for company.

However, is remote work only for white-collar IT workers? Importantly, will remote work further increase the fault lines between white- and blue-collar workers, as some reports seem to suggest? These are some questions that need to be examined.

McKinsey undertook an interesting analysis of 2000 tasks in 800 jobs spread over nine countries to estimate the potential of jobs and sectors in lending themselves to remote work. In their estimation, even in sectors like construction, warehousing, transportation, manufacturing, mining and retail trade, up to 20 per cent of the work can potentially be done remotely. Of course, sectors like financial services, management, professional, scientific and technical services, as well as IT, lend to much higher remote-work possibilities—in the range of 60–85 per cent.[2]

Today it is possible to drive forklifts without being at the construction site, perform surgeries without being at the operating theatre, test drug samples without being at the laboratory or till farms without being in the field. The power of technology has made not only IT and white-collar jobs tech-enabled but has also started impacting many sectors to allow for offsite remote work.

In my conversations with senior leaders at Tata Steel, a behemoth in steel manufacturing and supply in India, it came to light that in the throes of the pandemic, one of the many measures undertaken to ensure social distancing was to mirror 'pits' for the supervisors. Done with the help of cameras that recreated the pits, it enabled them to supervise work seamlessly. With the withdrawal of the pandemic, it stood to reason that the task the supervisors could oversee while sitting 10 metres away from the work site could also be undertaken when they were 10 kms or even 100 kms away.

Tata Steel is not alone in this. Unilever too has used the new virtual technologies to reimagine its production and manufacturing facilities. By creating 'global virtual operations room' to remotely monitor production, the company was able to synergize operations across 200 manufacturing sites across the world.[3]

Technologies such as digital twinning are already driving innovation and improving performance in manufacturing and other sectors. Digital twins can, in fact, replicate many real-world objects, from single pieces of equipment in a factory to full installations allowing the overseeing of the performance of an asset, identification of potential faults and a lot more.

A Deloitte report modeled the jobs of managers and engineers of tomorrow by reimagining what manufacturing jobs in the future could look like: digital twin engineer, robot teaming coordinator, drone data coordinator and smart factory manager. Interestingly, the smart factory manager's day begins with dropping his children to school while looking at the real-time location of a materials delivery truck on his car console. His day progresses with asking the 3D lab to deliver an inspection-ready prototype, coordinating with the robot teaming coordinator, running simulations with the after-market sales team, checking the predictive maintenance page to ensure all use cases are working well, and finalizing quality models and more before being reminded to be at his daughter's dance recital at 6 p.m.[4]

This, increasingly, will be the future of factory work, breaking all the rigidities that it stood for decades. Let us look at some of the other ways in which technology is enabling flexibility in traditional work and sectors.

Telepresence

Technology is in fact aiding people to do all kinds of physical work from a distance—whether it is surgery or seeding. Picture this: In a busy shopping district, a 24/7 convenience store is being tended to by a humanoid robot. It isn't attending to customers but working at keeping its shelves stocked. The robot, in turn, is being controlled by a remote worker, wearing a virtual reality set, who could well be an employee with limited mobility and who otherwise couldn't have stocked shelves unassisted.

Telepresence is also helping countries with severe workforce shortages by freeing people from the restrictions of distance and time. Key examples of the usage of telepresence include doctors performing surgery remotely or start-ups remotely controlling delivery as well as inspection of goods. Telepresence offers technicians the opportunity to undertake repairs from a remote location. An aircraft mechanic, for example, can simply don a Google Glass headset and stream what he sees to an expert and, with instructions received from the expert, easily accomplish a complex repair. Consider this like sharing your laptop screen, except that what you are sharing here is an activity from the real world.

Teleoperation

Teleoperation technology is yet another important step in taking the job to the person, as opposed to physically bringing the person to the job. Heavy-equipment maker Caterpillar, for example, is developing remote-controlled earthmovers. Being marketed as safety technology, they ensure that humans don't have to work in hazardous work environments.[5] Going forward, be it construction or road work, it could all be done away from the actual site, and in fact from within the four walls of an apartment. Similarly, airplanes, trains and automobiles could be controlled remotely. There could be excavator truck drivers who would not be required to leave their desks as they exercise driving control by means of a joystick or steering wheel while multiple monitors offer them a wide field of view.

Similarly, Teleo, a start-up in the teleoperation space in the US, specializes in retrofitting construction equipment so they can be operated remotely. Not only does it mean having fewer people on-site, it also means improving the quality of life for the driver and making his or her role safer. Speaking of safety, a project at the US Army Research Laboratory involves deployment of human teleoperators to train a reconnaissance robot how to drive across a tough terrain.

BCG, the well-known strategic management consulting group, has identified other important use cases for teleoperation:

✓ Big data-driven quality control that could pinpoint ways to minimize product failures and waste while reducing the number of workers specializing in quality control.

✓ Robot-assisted production that significantly reduces the amount of manual labour in production operations.

✓ Self-driving logistics vehicles that reduce the need for logistics personnel on site.

✓ Smart supply networks that reduce the requirement of on-site personnel in operations planning.

✓ Predictive maintenance that enables real-time remote monitoring of equipment.

✓ Augmented work, maintenance and service that makes use of augmented reality glasses to see dispatch information.

Clearly, among other things, the use of remote access systems, remote monitoring and remote notifications takes away the need to 'assemble' people physically in and around workspaces. A remote access system is, in fact, formed by integrating technologies such as supervisory control and data acquisition (SCADA), microcontrollers, open platform communications (OPC) servers, the Internet, and sensors and actuators that facilitate the control and monitoring of manufacturing operations remotely. Remote monitoring uses distributed control systems and SCADA systems for monitoring automated processes and systems. Remote notifications not only eliminate the need for additional people but also reduce unplanned downtime.

Overall, the shift to remote working can be enabled by adequate training to ensure collaboration between virtual and onsite workers.

Little surprise, then, that the research and advisory firm Gartner has predicted that 'half of all factory work will be done remotely, with hourly workers only needed onsite to perform certain tasks. Technologies such as the Internet of Things, Augmented Reality and Artificial Intelligence will enable engineers to have more insight into processes and machine performance than ever before'. [6]

The management consultancy McKinsey's 2020 report also found that Industry 4.0 technologies had helped to keep industry operations running during the worst phase of the pandemic.[7] Of course, it was the firms that had already scaled up their technological capabilities before the pandemic that were best placed to respond during the crisis.

Industry 4.0 is at an inflection point in India.

The Indian manufacturing sector is rapidly modernizing and embracing the Industry 4.0 (and 5.0) framework. Industry reports suggest that Indian manufacturing could have spent $5–6 billion on new technologies. One of the trends to watch out for would be the building of smart factories that can be connected globally, adding intelligence to synergize multi-locational facilities. One clear implication would be employment of skilled personnel from off-site locations in certain functions, such that they may need to migrate to the site where manufacturing is located. This opens up the possibilities we have been discussing so far.

Are remote blue-collar jobs only to do with high-end technology?

Not necessarily. Enough and more examples abound, of remote work facilitating the taking of opportunities to where talent exists.

The argan oil cooperatives in Morocco are one example. A key process in the extraction of argan oil is the cracking of the nut without destroying the kernel, a task that is done manually. The work is undertaken by mostly uneducated rural women from very small villages who work from home on their own schedules while also tending to their families. The impact of these kind of work-from-home opportunities in elevating the economy of these villages cannot be overstated.

Constructing parts of buildings in different localities and shipping them to other localities for on-site assembly will also be a new reality in times to come. In this context, it's worth recalling how China built a 1000-bed hospital in ten days during the Covid-19 pandemic. Based on media reports, it appears to consist in creating prefabricated units and building foundations in parallel, in a smart bid to avoid sequential processing and to execute with speed. A lot of this is possible because of the use of new-age technologies, even in an industry as traditional as construction.

Now imagine extending this same example back home, where the work might involve a mason in Champaran, Bihar. He may not be required to step out of his hometown as his wares could simply be transported to upscale Gurgaon. The implications of such developments for large-scale urban migration in India are huge.

We are lately seeing the fallouts of the existence of overly populated clusters all over the world, with countries like Japan even going to the extent of offering monetary incentives to move people out of Tokyo. A robust ecosystem that supports remote work is a very efficient answer to ease population pressures in big cities across the world.

To sum up

While we're all absorbed in discussions around remote white-collar jobs, a remote work revolution is slowly but surely taking the world of blue-collar workers by storm. Most jobs so far considered impossible to be undertaken remotely can become remote with the right technology, as also with some creative thinking. With 'tech' appended to many traditional sectors—like edtech, healthtech, foodtech and more—the traditional distinction between tech and non-tech jobs has been in any case blurring. There are, therefore, several domains that are throwing up jobs that can be done from anywhere.

It will be a worthwhile exercise to look at some burgeoning sectors in India—such as retail, which employs as many as 35 million people—which lend themselves to remote work. In fact, a Nasscom report says the Indian retail sector is likely to generate as many as 25 million new jobs by 2030, a lion's share of which will come from the offline-online model.[8] Even a back-of-the-envelope calculation as to how many remote jobs such sectors can create in rural areas shows that we could be talking about a few million over the next decade. What is more, the blue-collar remote trend will expand the labour pool for companies while also offering opportunities to rural communities and others, who would otherwise be left out of the workforce.

It's time, therefore, for both the government and forward-thinking companies to create new-age employment models for blue-collar employees. Implemented correctly, they can bridge the gap between India and Bharat and help build a far more inclusive India. It is inclusion of blue-collar work that builds a strong case for a national strategy around remote work in India. Only bold experiments can help build inclusive human capital and drive higher employment.

In the following chapter, let us look at how promotion of greater human capital inclusion can address some of the gaps between Bharat and India imaginatively.

6

Human Capital Inclusion

India's Exceptional Opportunity

A rising tide lifts every boat[1] *. . . but while some sip champagne in a yacht, others struggle to keep their raft afloat.*[2]

Desam ante matti kadoye, desam ante manushuloye (A nation is not its land, a nation is its people)—so goes the English translation of what the famous Telugu poet Gurazada Appa Rao said in his inimitable Telugu.[3] As the world's most populous nation, India's most important asset is its people. We must learn to make capital out of this vast population by investing in them to improve their knowledge, skills and personality. This is when our demography will start giving the much-anticipated dividend. The potential to unleashing human capital, in this context, is India's most distinctive and exceptional opportunity.

But sometimes it feels as though human capital is an afterthought for our policymakers, both at the firm and national government levels. I am referring not to the visible rhetoric of 'people are our greatest asset', but to the reality behind it. We think of many levers of growth—financial, infrastructure development, technology, market access, etc.—but always before we think of people. It is assumed that if we get all these right, people will somehow follow and step up.

In this chapter, I argue that human capital must be thought of first, and ahead of all other strategies for sustainable national growth and development. For this, we must think beyond traditional 'inclusive growth' and conceptualize human capital inclusion as a prerequisite to economic growth.

To the best of my knowledge, 'human capital inclusion' is not a commonly used expression. Of course, the ideas of human capital and inclusion separately exist—ironically, somewhat in mutual exclusion. Inspired by the buzz around financial inclusion, I propose that we join these two ideas together and build human capital inclusion as a powerful socio-economic construct and deploy it in policymaking. I trace my thoughts to the very origins of human capital theory. Let me explain:

Several different forms of capital have received attention from scholars and practitioners over time. The ones that are often part of the public discourse include financial capital, structural capital, intellectual capital, social capital and human capital. While all these forms of capital overlap and interact with each other, they are often strategic to the functioning of a firm and to the success of nations too. Among these, human capital stands out as a resource that impacts and catalyses all other forms of capital. However, as it turns out, all humans are not capital. Only when humans acquire relevant and useful skills, knowledge and abilities do they become useful as capital. Whether we like it or not, this is the gross capitalist view on human beings—a resource to be utilized in the overall economic activities of the society. Whether or not we should take such a narrow view, given the vast potential that is associated with human beings, would be a subject for another book altogether.

The capital/economic view of human beings is typically ascribed to Gary Becker, a Nobel laureate who is often regarded as the 'father of human capital'. In his prolific and illustrious career, he developed what he would later call 'the economic approach to human behaviour'. It is his research in this area that led to the publication of the book *Human Capital*. The book is Becker's classic study of how investment in an individual's education and training is similar to making business investments in equipment, for example.

In Becker's words:

> To most people capital means a bank account, a hundred shares of IBM stock, assembly lines, or steel plants in the Chicago area. These are all forms of capital in the sense that they are assets that yield income and other useful outputs over long periods of time. But these tangible forms of capital are not the only ones—schooling, a computer training course, expenditures of medical care, and lectures on the virtues of punctuality and honesty also are capital. That is because they raise earnings, improve health, or add to a person's good habits over much of his lifetime.[4]

It is this investment in human capital that has been the driver of the knowledge economy, as it centres on the idea that investments in people, such as education, increase in worker productivity and skill sets lead to the formation of human capital. The theory highlights the common assertion that the more educated a person becomes, the more valuable he or she will be for their specific knowledge and the greater their human capital.

While the human capital theory stands to reason, it needs to come with an important caveat—namely, that all humans, who are capital, may not come by the same opportunities to use their capital or gain from it. What holds people from becoming valuable, like capital, or from using their capital for further growth, is the lack of barrier-free access to opportunities.

The overall discourse on inclusion has taken many shapes; more recently there has been a proposal for a distributive framework that ensures greater equity in sharing the benefits of growth. The Organisation for Economic Co-operation and Development's (OECD) Framework for Policy Action on Inclusive Growth (a comprehensive reference document in this area) moves beyond GDP metrics and statistical averages to 'focus on equity, people, and well-being and emphasizes the *distribution* of opportunities and outcomes to create sustainable growth'.[5]

OECD, the well-known intergovernmental body headquartered in Paris, France, in their above report recommend that *'equality needs to be considered from the start when governments design growth policies, rather than tackled afterward through redistribution. Such an ex-ante approach can help people, firms and regions fulfil their potential and drive growth, both locally and globally'.*[6]

As we trace the origins of the theory of equitable distribution, we find that it emanated from development economists' frustration with the famous 'trickle-down theory' of growth. Rafael Ranieri and Raquel Almeida

Ramos at the International Policy Centre for Inclusive Growth (IPC-IG) have tracked the evolution of this concept of inclusive growth. They explain rather lucidly how, initially, economists thought growth and equity cannot coexist and argued that growth might cause temporary inequality.[7]

However, over time, as the benefits of growth trickle down, all get to benefit from the growth. It was Simon Kuznets, an American economist and statistician, who initially hypothesized that as an economy develops, market forces first increase then decrease the overall economic inequality in a society, as illustrated by the well-known inverted U-shaped Kuznets curve.[8]

The hypothesis states that in the early development of an economy, there are new investment opportunities where people who already hold wealth can increase that wealth. This stage sees an increase in economic inequality. However, that same economic inequality is expected to decrease at a certain stage of development, when the processes associated with industrialization, such as democratization and the development of a welfare state, take hold. It is at this point in economic development that society is meant to benefit from what is known as the trickle-down effect.

Over time, development economists disagreed with this view, especially since in many parts of the world, more notably in developing countries, economic growth did not always lead to fair and equitable growth. This eventually led to the view that the distribution of income post surges of growth needs to be consciously integrated into policy, as opposed to be left to chance.

In this context, we see a virtuous interdependence between inclusion and growth. While conventional thinking believes that you need to grow first and include later, the fact is that we can't grow unless we 'include' ex-ante. In fact, we must first include people (human capital) in our pursuit of growth and only then can we grow to find enough resources to distribute the benefits of growth. Hence, the proposition that inclusion is an antecedent of growth and not its consequence. This belief places inclusion ahead of growth as a prerequisite for growth, which can lead to a new mindset of 'inclusion for growth', as different from 'inclusive growth'.

With this new understanding, we need to look at how India's vast human capital is not being included adequately as an engine of growth, as opposed to being considered the beneficiary of growth. Nobel-prize-winning economist Amartya Sen's perspective on human capital extends beyond the traditional economic measures. He argues, 'Development consists of the removal of various types of unfreedoms that leave people with little choice and little opportunity of exercising their reasoned agency.'[9]

What, then, are some of the factors coming in the way of this lack of inclusion, or as Amartya Sen says 'unfreedoms', and what can we do about them?

Unequal access to foundational education

That there is unequal access to education in India is a given. As per the Economic Survey, the gross enrolment ratio (GER) in higher education was recorded at 27.3 per cent in FY21. Additionally, there was a high incidence of dropouts.[10] Unified District Information System for Education Plus (UDISE+) data shows that the dropout rate is highest at the secondary school level (standards 9 to

10), at 12.6 per cent.[11] The dropout rate is higher for girls than for boys at all levels of education. Independent studies have also noted a spike in rural school dropout rates and a widening digital divide during and post the pandemic. The pandemic has further exacerbated and amplified the challenges in education, such as access, continuity and learning gaps. The long-term consequences of such non-inclusion cannot be overemphasized, as they have serious economic and societal ramifications. We must work towards preventing students from dropping out of school and ensure that children—especially from vulnerable groups, girls, tribal communities and minority or migrating groups, etc.—receive quality education. In fact, inclusive growth demands that we aspire towards 100 per cent completion of secondary education for all citizens of the country.

The other equally important aspect has to do with ensuring that access to schooling also translates into learning. While we have attempted to provide universal access to elementary education, the foundational literacy and numeracy skills of many children are still very low, particularly among disadvantaged groups. According to the Annual Status of Education Report (ASER) a publication of ASER Center, a unit of Pratham, the well-known school-education not-for-profit that sheds light on learning outcomes in schools, only 27.2 per cent of Class III students could read a simple Class II-level text, and only 28.1 per cent could do basic subtraction in 2018.[12] Clearly, foundational learning is a critical gap in India that needs sectoral reforms. It calls for a nationwide mission with a holistic approach; one that will improve literacy and also focus on finding solutions and develop cost-effective and technology-driven interventions.

It is only with widespread quality education that we can hope to break the vicious cycle of unemployment and poverty.

Poor plumbing between skills and employability

While education is a necessary prerequisite for employability, what is also important is that this education translates into industry-relevant skills. As things stand today, the plumbing is poor in the matter of translation of education into skills. What this requires is a granular understanding of employment readiness. While the rising unemployment in India is attributed to a shortage of jobs in the country, the fact is that a huge number of companies in India report shortage of talented employees. According to Manpower Group's report 'Talent Shortage 2020', a whopping 63 per cent of companies in India reported a shortage of talented employees, mainly in IT, engineering services and sales.[13] The National Employability Report for Engineers 2019 put out by Aspiring Minds, the job assessment platform, has shown that over 80 per cent of engineers in India are unfit to take up any job in the knowledge economy.[14] The Wheebox India Skills Report 2023 suggests that only about 50.3 per cent of young people in the country were found to be highly employable.[15] Employers seek a diverse set of domain skills, ranging from the functional to the technical, and there emerges India's glaring skills gap. Clearly, theoretical knowledge is not enough. The need of the hour is experiential learning, mentoring and industry apprenticeship. Besides job readiness, as defined by socio-emotional skills, work ethics and culture, communication and collaboration, etc., need to be taught too, along with domain skills. Currently, though, these job-readiness skills are not getting the required structured interventions on a priority basis.

The National Education Policy 2020, is being seen as an important step that is slated to change the face of the Indian educational system. The new policy rightly emphasizes transitioning from the current learning-based approach to a skill-based model. Implemented well, it can transform the market significantly and cater to the evolving needs of employers.[16]

In addition to implementing the NEP, what is also needed is a change in the Indian mindset when it comes to vocational education. To this end, a national brand and communication campaign (much like the family planning campaign in the 1970s and the Swachh Bharat or anti-tobacco campaigns of the current times) to position skills and vocations as being 'hip' and happening is the need of the hour. Clearly, India's next generation of career and occupational choices must move away from the colonial mindset of preference for status and authority alone, or worse still, government jobs.

Wage parity and competitiveness

Let us face it, it is the wage differentials too that are punishing for people and keep them from making real career choices. Sample this: a dentist, after five to seven years of education on average, starts with a monthly salary as low as Rs 25,000. At the same time Uber drivers and food delivery executives sometimes earn more than a trained dentist does. What explains this irony? There are enough and more examples of such wage asymmetries. Teachers, for instance, especially those that teach in private schools, are known to survive on a pittance. It is not surprising that the teaching profession no longer attracts the best talent.

The need of the hour is not just governmental policies but also industry-level action. It is about time employers begin to look at salaries not just as avoidable costs but as a thoughtful investment in attracting and utilizing appropriate talent.

Once education and skills are addressed and equal opportunities are created for all—not as reservations but as proactive, affirmative and remedial actions with a mindset of 'inclusion as growth', a spiral of goodwill will be unleashed. More and more people will find ways to equip themselves to participate in the labour market. In short, human capital in the country will be unleashed to its full potential.

What is needed is the creation of a level playing field and equal access to employment opportunities for participants in the labour market. While reservations, government jobs and rural employment schemes are all fine in their own place, they lack the broad sweep of 'inclusion', which is a force multiplier.

Inclusion of women

The proactive inclusion of women in economic activity is a great example of the power of inclusion. There have been enough and more research reports showing us that increased inclusion of women in the workforce is crucial to economic growth. Ironically, however, in the Indian context, women's employment rate, which had peaked at 35 per cent in 2004, fell to around 25 per cent in 2022.[17] The Centre for Monitoring the Indian Economy (CMIE), which uses a more restrictive definition of employment, found that in 2022 only 10 per cent of working-age Indian women were either employed or looking for jobs. No surprise, then, that the contribution of women to India's GDP is 18 per cent, one of the lowest proportions in the world.

According to McKinsey Global Institute's recent report, more than 70 per cent of potential GDP opportunity comes from increasing women's participation in the labour force by 10 percentage points. The report states, 'India has one of the largest opportunities in the world to boost GDP by advancing women's equality – $770 billion of added GDP by 2025.'[18]

It is clear for us to see that with adequate inclusion of women and other such marginalized groups, we could be looking at dynamic engines of growth that can propel India to its $5-trillion economy target and far beyond.

To sum up

It is only when human capital is prepared, included and deployed that economic growth will accelerate. We have put the cart before the horse and are waiting for growth to happen first and then to include people who can benefit from it. While this is true of the financial inclusion model, which can centre on distribution of the benefits of growth, human capital inclusion, on the other hand, is about investing in the growth of people ahead of investing in the growth of the economy.

In the following chapter, we will look at yet another exceptional and unique opportunity that India has—the untapped potential of its small cities and towns, or 'Bharat', as it is popularly referred to.

7

'Bharat'

The Future of India

*It is fine for urban and rural areas to be different.
Difference is fine. Disparity is not.*[1]

Some of us would recall a campaign launched in 2007 to
mark the sixtieth year of Indian independence. Named
'India Poised' and launched by the *Times of India*, it
showcased India's achievements in megastar Amitabh
Bachchan's baritone:
The lines of the campaign ran as below:

There are two Indias in this country. One India is
straining at the leash, eager to spring forth and live up
to all the adjectives that the world has been showering
recently upon us. The other India is in the leash. One
India says give me a chance and I will prove myself. The
other India says, prove yourself first and maybe then
you will have a chance. One India lives in the optimism

of our hearts. The other India lurks in the scepticism of our minds. One India wants. The other India hopes. One India leads, the other India follows. But conversions are on the rise each passing day. And more people from the other India are coming over to this side.

The campaign drew attention to an India poised for great things but held back by some. Traditionally, this is how India has been viewed, the richer urban centres as India and Bharat as its poorer cousin. While India was generally perceived to be the land of skyscrapers, luxury vehicles, technology parks, tech unicorns and more, Bharat was seen as that rural and semi-urban hinterland with the tiniest of landholdings and people who were unskilled and lived below the poverty line.

Times, however, are definitely changing, and so is Bharat. In fact, if one can take the liberty of slightly amending a statement made by Mahatma Gandhi—Real India lives in its villages—one can say that 'the future of India lies in its small towns'. Increasingly, every piece of research seems to be making clear that it is 'Bharat' that will provide the next growth spurt for the country. Many studies are suggesting that Bharat is indeed the new rising India.

Before we delve deep into this, it is important to understand that 'Bharat' is primarily a media coinage. There are, of course, many myths associated with this part of the country that big city 'India' often looks down on disparagingly. One of the myths that needs to be debunked early is that Bharat is unskilled and illiterate. Interestingly, when we look at Bharat in terms of India's first Internet users, we find that Internet users in Bharat are over-indexed on education compared with Internet users in India overall.[2] Speaking of Internet usage per se, it is estimated that of the 759 million Internet users in 2022, 399 million were in rural India, as opposed to 360 million in urban India. The total number is expected to reach 900 million by 2025, where 56 per cent of all new Internet users are estimated to be from rural India. It is also estimated that by 2025, 65 per cent of all new Internet users will be women.[3]

A 2019 report from Google titled 'Year in Search: Insights for Brands' points out that consumers in the non-metros increasingly use online services to search for information regarding insurance, beauty and travel more than in the metros. Over 70 per cent of all smartphone-related searches come from small towns, while 61 per cent of all searches for banking and financial services and 55 per cent of auto-related searches are coming from the non-metros.[4] The difference between 'India' and 'Bharat', is therefore not as simplistic as that one is urban and shining and the other rural and drowning.

In fact, one needs to recognize that several tiers of economy exist in India today. What were traditionally dismissed as smaller, underdeveloped cities and towns are now rising up the ranks in connectivity, amenities and access. These cities now boast of improved infrastructure, quicker Internet access, better transport, communication and more. A recent study by Ambit Capital on the so-called 'middle cities'—the fifteen cities that follow India's top eight metros—found that 'Incomes in middle cities are likely to be growing faster than that of the top-8, and in absolute terms incomes could be two times that of other smaller cities.'[5] It may come as a pleasant surprise to many that a recent report by Oxford Economics, a UK-based global forecasting and quantitative analysis firm, says that all ten of the world's fastest-growing cities between 2019 and 2035 are predicted to be in India. In fact, as many as seventeen of the top twenty cities on the list will be Indian. Interestingly, the list includes a number of tier-2 cities, such as Surat, Rajkot, Agra, Nagpur, Tiruppur, Vijayawada and Tiruchirappalli.[6] Speaking of tier-2 cities, Chandigarh, Jaipur, Ahmedabad, Kochi, Thiruvananthapuram, Lucknow, Indore, Bhubaneshwar, Visakhapatnam and Coimbatore are slated to emerge as the new growth cities of India, in terms of retail consumption as well as office space leasing, says an analysis by CBRE, a leading property consultancy.[7] Similarly, a survey carried out by IIM Ahmedabad indicates that tier-2 cities are bigger spenders per purchase online than their metro counterparts (cite). In fact, e-shoppers from tier-2 cities spend up to 60 per cent more than metro shoppers. Little surprise, then, that Flipkart, Amazon, Zepto, Ecom Express, Mahindra Logistics and Transport Corporation of India are ramping up their delivery, logistics and warehouse workforce in the non-metros, going by media reports.

A recent media report quoted Myntra top executives as stating that tier-2 markets contribute up to 40 per cent of their sales during mega sales events, and that small towns could account for more than half of the company's sales in the next three or four years.[8] Amazon's founder and former chief executive officer Jeff Bezos has spoken of Amazon localizing its strategy to make its offerings attractive to India.[9] Walmart Chief Executive Officer Doug McMillon has also waxed eloquent on how kirana stores would be central to Walmart's operations in India.[10]

Tier-2 cities have also seen an increase in not just online sales but also offline stores of brands such as Birkenstock, Uniqlo and Tim Hortons. Fast-food chains like McDonald's, traditionally known to have an urban foothold, are also setting up in cities such as Salem, Erode and Belagavi. Reports also show small towns accounting for 40–50 per cent of sales of several premium direct-to-consumer (D2C) brands across categories, such as grooming and beauty, wellness foods and wearables. According to Kantar Worldpanel's (an international market research and analytics group) shopper analysis report for FY22, Indian small towns with populations of less than 10 lakh have also led growth for baby-care items like diapers, lotions and feed formulations, while the demand for these goods in metro markets actually de-grew.[11] Driven by first-time consumers, brands such as boAt, Bombay Shaving Company, Wonderchef and Mamaearth have reportedly been placing their bets on small towns.

This change is clearly driven by rising aspirations. The chairman of Nestle, the fast-moving consumer goods firm, was recently quoted as saying that the company is witnessing rural markets aspirationally emulating urban India and that it is on a path to accelerated growth in rural areas.[12] Analyse any sector and you are likely to witness a similar story. Rural markets accounted for as high as 43.6 per cent of sales for the car maker Maruti Suzuki in 2021-22. Italian automaker Automobili Lamborghini is tapping smaller centres in India to generate additional volumes. Cities such as Surat and Ludhiana are already among the top ten markets for luxury cars in India.

Studying abroad, yet another aspirational marker, is also showing a skew towards smaller markets, as students from small towns make a beeline for foreign universities. In a study by Prodigy Finance, study-abroad loan applications reported a 98 per cent growth in the first quarter of 2022 from the corresponding period the previous year.

Interestingly, tier-2 and tier-3 cities contributed sizeably to this growth.[13]

Speaking of financial indicators, Zerodha, a large online stock brokerage, has been reporting that several demat accounts have been opened from small towns and tier-2 and tier-3 cities. Fifty-six per cent of Bharat users are known to complete their monetary transactions through net banking and online debit card transactions. Not only that, 49 per cent of them use mobile wallets. Bharat users are also seen to be quite aware about mutual funds, cryptocurrency and other new-age investments.[14]

With improved awareness, better connectivity and the rising level of financial inclusion, Bharat has become an important sub-text in every marketer's strategic arsenal, be it an FMCG company like Hindustan Lever or a more primarily urban-focused brand like McDonalds.

Interestingly, Bharat is also home to the new startup culture. No surprise there, as Ambit's study found. In their ratio of graduates, the middle cities are comparable to the big metros.[15] A media report says funding for small town start-ups grew 41 per cent in 2022, while in big cities like Mumbai and Bengaluru, startup funding saw a dip of 48 per cent in the corresponding period.[16] Ritesh Agarwal of Oyo was quoted in the 2022 Global Unicorn Summit as saying, 'The rapid evolution of internet infrastructure, allowing cheap and quick distribution at scale, combined with access to capital provides the opportunity for a large number of small businesses in the country to scale up and become high quality sizable companies.'

Other than from the financial indicators, the growing confidence of Bharat is also seen in many other aspects, a strong example being the pushback by rural citizens against the farm laws. Interestingly, therefore, public policy towards Bharat is also changing. The Union Budget, for example, lays a lot of emphasis on hitherto ignored sectors such as small-scale industry and the farm sector. In fact, experts have noticed a marked emphasis on collapsing the India-Bharat divide in the Union Budget 2023.

Importantly, along with the changes in consumption, what we are also witnessing is a big cultural shift when it comes to small-town India. A new breed of 'Bharat social media influencers' is emerging as a natural corollary of the focus on this large catchment area.[17]

Popular media such as films and OTT series are also increasingly focusing on small towns as their story settings, which speaks volumes about the rising interest in Bharat.

Battle for talent needs to play out in small towns

These are all heartening changes, to say the least. What is critical, however, is for these changes to be ubiquitous and not be restricted to the elite in these towns and villages. For that to happen, India Inc. will need to step up its game and play a key role. To start with, the go-to bias of employers needs to shift from tier-1 cities to address the burgeoning aspirations of these next towns-to-be-cities, like Salem, Jhansi, Gwalior, Vijayawada, Rajahmundry, Meerut, Mathura, Bhatinda, Bikaner, Cuttack, Madurai, Baroda, Nashik and Tiruchirappalli, which are brimming with talent. In digital skills too, some of the smaller towns are already taking the lead. Survey reports say that Ahmedabad and Jaipur are 'leaders' in both total and digital talent. Mysuru, surprisingly, has a higher density of digital talent than many other cities because of the location of advanced training facilities there. Many smaller towns like Warangal, Kanpur, Nashik, Hubbali and Tiruchirappalli are rapidly emerging as hubs for digital talent.[18]

To grow and nurture local talent in these cities and provide them the necessary infrastructure, the government has drawn up many programmes. The Aspirational Districts Programme, a government initiative by NITI Aayog started in 2018 for example, marks an important shift in the approach towards inclusive development by focusing on critical areas like skill development, healthcare, education, agriculture, water resources, financial inclusion and basic infrastructure. As many as 112 'Aspirational Districts' across twenty-seven states have been identified, and steps are being taken to make these areas socially, economically and physically sustainable. A lot more, however, needs to be done where employment generation is concerned.

The Shyama Prasad Mukherji Rurban Mission (SPMRM) started in 2016, similarly, strives to strengthen rural areas by providing economic, social and infrastructure amenities, endeavouring to lead to sustainable and balanced regional development in the country. The vision of SPMRM is to 'develop a cluster of villages that preserve and nurture the essence of rural community life with focus on equity, and inclusiveness, without compromising with the facilities perceived to be essentially urban in nature, thus creating a cluster of Rurban villages'.[19] The larger outcomes envisaged under this mission are to bridge the rural-urban divide and attract investments in rural areas. Unfortunately, we are yet to see any breakthrough in this mission.

These steps notwithstanding, we still have a long way to go to make sure that Bharat and India do not remain two separate realities. In the following chapter, we will look at how remote work can become a big enabler for Bharat. It will go a long way in not only fuelling the country's economy and making an atmanirbhar Bharat a reality, but it will also add to the country's global heft. It is about time that jobs followed talent instead of jobseekers having to chase urban office-centric jobs. Accomplishing this will ensure human capital inclusion and address the divide between Bharat and India, an urgent need.

In the next chapter, we discuss how, by intentionally shaping and choosing the *future of work* options like remote work, we will be able to take more jobs to Bharat from urban India.

8

Shaping the *Future of Work* for Bharat and India

India's way is not Europe's. India is not Calcutta and Bombay. India lives in her seven hundred thousand villages.

—Mahatma Gandhi[1]

India's future as an IT superpower was built way back in the 1980s. Then not so well-known IT services companies such as TCS and Infosys built a hugely successful outsourcing model based on offshore delivery. They could convince discerning clients in Europe and the US that distance did not matter, nor location. Being based in Bengaluru or Mumbai—seven seas away, as they say—from their clients, they proved that co-location is not mandatory for successful delivery of IT services. India's claim to fame as the IT hub of the world would not have been possible if their Western counterparts did not trust Indians to work from their hometowns.

However, when it comes to work within India, the same model is met with hesitation. Whereas someone in Boston trusted work to happen from Bengaluru, we in Bengaluru do not trust that it can happen from Belagavi. Come to think of it, why should there be a need for talent from Guntur or Munnar to travel to Gurgaon or Mumbai? It is exactly here that we can shape, steer and leverage the *future of work* to take work to Bharat from India.

Professor Michael Lipton, who specialized in the study of rural poverty in developing countries, has observed: 'The most important class conflict in the poor countries of the world today is not between labour and capital. Nor is it between foreign and national interests. It is between the rural and urban classes.'[2] For this theory to be put into practice, we need a mindset change among employers. Employers need to overcome their ingrained biases against rural folk and display the willingness to tweak employment models so that they are location-agnostic. Importantly, with such a focus, there will be added opportunities for women, people with different abilities and senior citizens, enabling them to be part of the active workforce. Apart from remote work options, employment models like creation of satellite centres, colocation of spaces or sometimes the taking of work itself to newer towns can be flexible arrangements. Providing structured hybrid work arrangements and giving employees the option to travel to the nearby big towns periodically will further add to flexibility for the workforce. All this will address the gap between the small towns and big cities. Flexible work options will open up more doors, especially to women, whom we badly need in our workforce. Raghuram Rajan, noted economist and former Reserve Bank of India governor, and his co-author Rohit Lamba, assistant professor of economics at

Pennsylvania State University, recommend part-time jobs for women and ask employers to offer 'alternative job structures, flexible hours, and shared responsibilities . . . through half-day jobs'. They urge the Indian government to 're-examine labor and tax regulations that stand in the way of creating part-time jobs and create some itself'.[3]

Country roads take me home

The testing times of the pandemic, when professionals headed to their hometowns in the face of stringent lockdowns, stand testimony to the immense pain caused by mandating locations for work. A random scanning of news reports from the immediate period after the pandemic suggests that more than 20 per cent of big city-based employees moved back to close to 200 unique small and big towns—and many of them are continuing there.

Forward-thinking companies, of course, continue to tap into the vast potential for expansion of their talent pool as they look at small cities for talent that is cost-effective, stable and reliable. Indian tier-2 cities, such as Chandigarh, Vadodara, Indore, Coimbatore, Kochi and Trivandrum, have become key employment hubs in the IT sector, and approximately seventy global in-house centres based in India have expanded into tier-2 locations and are expected to see enormous growth.[4] Such 'hub and spoke' models, where there are micro-offices across the country rather than just a few large set-ups, could give Bharat the impetus it needs.

At one time the technology major HCL even ran a 'come back home' campaign, encouraging local talent to take up opportunities in their hometowns. The 'stay rooted' campaign focused on creating global opportunities for graduates in their home cities. Speaking of offering new opportunities to freshers spread across the country in another context, my conversation with Suresh Tripathi, former chief human resources officer at Air India and now adviser to them, brought to light how the airline is consciously looking at recruiting young talent from far-flung areas of the country and training them extensively in multidisciplinary approaches to take up cabin crew jobs. Suresh told me that over 2400 such young people are already in various stages of training and will soon 'take flight'. What we need are several such industry-wide endeavours.

The green shoots

The rise of agri-tech platforms is empowering the agricultural sector, the mainstay of rural India, in interestingly new ways. Leveraging the power of AI, ML, IoT, remote sensing and other technologies, we can now build platforms to enable sustainable farming on a large scale. Such use of technologies will also create multiple blue-collar jobs and a gig-based ecosystem in rural India. Importantly, these agri-tech platforms can help build gender inclusiveness by bringing more women into the rural economy.

Among other things, the emergence of such platforms allow the rural youth to up-skill themselves remotely and be ready for future jobs. In turn, this will expand the talent pool away from the metros. By embracing the *future of work*, we will also adopt futuristic technologies, like 5G, artificial intelligence, cloud, robotic process automation, blockchain, IoT and advanced cyber security—all enabling a whole new shift to distributed working across cities and towns.

It is encouraging to see that some entrepreneurs are beginning to take their enterprises and jobs to rural India.

Having realized the efficacy of working remotely, they are now increasingly mindful of the fact that waking up to the sound of birds chirping in the countryside and the ambition to create a large enterprise are not either-or choices. It is heartening to note that 52 per cent of India's recognized start-ups were in the tier-2 and tier-3 cities as of 2022.[5]

The extraordinary Zoho story

India's home-grown Zoho, the $1-billion cloud software suite and SaaS application company, is one such story of opportunities being taken to where the talent is. The Zoho philosophy is that world-class products can be built from anywhere, even if it means working out of a farm in a remote town.

Overall, Zoho's pronounced focus is on 'technology-enabled' rural revival. It is leveraging cloud computing to tap into rural talent and create job opportunities for them. In doing so, it is giving back to local communities, which are often overlooked. Not only has Zoho been able to create jobs and nurture talent locally, it has also empowered villages to be self-reliant with deep tech know-how.

What adds credence to the Zoho story is that its CEO, Sridhar Vembu, has enough skin in the game. He himself has moved to a village in Tenkasi, Tamil Nadu, and has been running his software company out of there. His company clocked annual profits of $330 million in FY23.[6]

The Tenkasi model

At the community level, Zoho is one of the main reasons for Tenkasi being given district status. By bringing high-paying jobs to this small town, the community has seen a dramatic improvement in its economic welfare and stability. Some of the parameters of success of the Tenkasi model include improved education levels and improvement in the standard of living of the families of employees. It is extremely encouraging to also see social mores changing for the better, as Zoho has facilitated women of the district to be able to spend money on themselves and also make their own lifestyle decisions.

Zoho's official mission statement is: 'In five years, 50 per cent of our employees will work from smaller, rural centers. We want to keep people rooted in their towns and villages, and provide world-class jobs in these places.'[7]

Many other companies, too, are using the power of technology for the cause of rural entrepreneurship. The Fintech startup BANKIT, for example, has been harnessing resources in tier-2 and tier-3 towns as well as villages and promoting rural entrepreneurship. BANKIT has on-boarded thousands of 'Digi Mitras', who are at the forefront of rural entrepreneurship by delivering various BANKIT services. Similarly, Vegavid Technology, a digital transformation company headquartered in the greater New York area, has developed an application called 'MyRojgaar', which connects skilled/unskilled workers and businesses in India. These are just a few platforms that are top-of-the-mind names. There are many such online portals that connect rural youth with jobs.

Clearly, rural jobs will transform and rural wages will increase when we are able to open urban opportunities to rural residents. For this, we need to move work to the worker, as opposed to the worker to work. In the absence of these efforts, while we may be staring at a modest 7–8 per cent official unemployment rate In India, disguised unemployment will continue to gnaw at the rural ecosystem.

In my conversations with B.P. Biddappa, executive director, HUL, and chief people, transformation and sustainability officer, South Asia, it was extremely heartening to know that in setting up factories in rural areas, Unilever is also running a sustainable community development initiative, Prabhat, which builds on local community needs at the grassroots level. Having undertaken a baseline survey across all sites, the company has identified key employable skills that would be of value to the community. Prabhat's 'livelihood centres' are now bringing positive change by enhancing both employability and income generation among rural communities. Today, they conduct training in spoken English, beauty and hair care, tailoring, web and graphic design, laptop and mobile repair, welding and other skills. So far, over 1,30,000 people have been given skill-based training and have been certified.

Tata Steel, similarly, runs nine JNTVTI (J.N. Tata Vocational Training Institute) centres across their production sites in Jharkhand, Odisha and Maharashtra. Over 10,000 students have been trained in twenty-one different trades and placed in the last seven years. Through a curriculum that has been developed in-house, these institutes train rural folks and help generate employment for them. In fact, all the vendors of the company are offered added incentives should they hire people from these places. Zubin Palia, group chief human resources and industrial relations at Tata Steel, explained to me that the company's vision is to become the best skills supplier in the world.

Yes, there are a few and growing examples of big-company initiatives to create rural employment. But where is the large-scale evidence of the success of this model, you may ask. Clearly, the use case for taking work from India to Bharat will not come from asking who else has done it. Instead, it will come from challenging our deeply entrenched city-centred, office-centred view of work. This, in turn, will happen if we take an ecosystem view of the new model of technology-enabled remote work and not see it as a tactical policy around the privilege of working from home for a lucky few.

In the meantime, we do have some examples from across the world where radical attempts are being made to move work away from big cities to small towns. The small country of Croatia, with a population the size of the Indian city of Surat, is offering 'digital nomad visas' and encouraging large-city workers from overseas to come and stay for extended periods in the country.[8] On the other hand, as mentioned earlier, countries like Japan are putting money where their mouth is. They, in fact, offer 1 million yen per child to families, to encourage them to leave Tokyo in favour of rural areas.[9] It will be worthwhile to also mention that there are many such programmes already running in the US, in states like Oklahoma, Alabama and Kansas.

Back to India—my research has identified at least ten factors that can promote remote work. Interestingly, these factors are, in turn, influenced by a wider adoption of remote work. These include: i) Universal access to reliable broadband networks across India, ii) Urban decongestion, iii) Carbon emission control, iv) Commuting woes in the big cities, v) Rural living conditions and quality of life in small towns vi) Changes in employment and career models, vii) Willingness to hire from rural/small town talent, viii) Changes in managerial mindsets and approaches, ix) Changes in HR policies and processes, and x) Designing, building and leading new-age fluid organizations.

Each of the above factors should be examined from the point of view of what the *future of work* offers to countries like India. If we decide to integrate employment generation and rural development within the broader framework of the *future of work*, we will generate several new work opportunities. A lot more needs to be done both at the policy level and in terms of changing mindsets. As Biddappa of HUL says, 'We must break the umbilical cord of needing to see people assembled physically in a room.' Employers also need to make a lot of changes to their conventional HR systems and practices in the areas of sourcing, recruiting, training, monitoring and assessment of work, while overall engaging better with their workforce. It is through these changes that we will be able to shape the *future of work* to benefit Bharat.

If you think these changes are optional, you may be mistaken. While for the current generation of organizations these may look like unnecessary experiments, for the next generations these changes would be natural expectations. The next chapter will discuss in detail what Gen Z and the other generations that will follow will expect and demand from us to integrate Bharat with India. Since the next generations will constitute a big vote bank, it will also compel politicians to address the urgent issues of taking jobs to rural India and also creating jobs in the hinterland.

9

How Gen Z Will Demand and Drive the Flexibility Agenda

Every generation tailors history to its taste.

— Ada Louise Huxtable[1]

There are many perspectives, anecdotes, myths and misgivings around generational differences. Some like to believe that the labels of Gen X, Gen Y, Gen Z and the newly minted Gen Alpha are rather arbitrary. They argue that fundamental human needs remain the same and that every generation wants pretty much the same thing as the previous ones—namely, a good life. Well, not quite. There could be some common threads running across generations in some matters, but what constitutes a good life, for example, changes from generation to generation. Clearly, generational shifts in attitudes, preferences and expectations from work and life are real and tangible.

The world, in fact, is undergoing a major demographic upheaval, and there are key components to this: Population growth, changes in life expectancy and the associated changes in the age structure of the population. The focus on a new generation of the young workforce has become more urgent because of this significant demographic shift. Recently, India dethroned China as the world's most populous country when its population reached a whopping 1.42 billion. A UN analysis has indicated that India's population will continue to grow for the next three decades, till 2050.[2] According to the report, as high as 68 per cent of India's total population is between the ages of fifteen and sixty-four, which is considered the working-age population in most countries. Moreover, the median age in India will be under thirty-four for the next decade. This will signal a 'paradigm shift' for India's development. While ageing populations may place additional strains on healthcare and other welfare systems in other countries, India's population clearly comes with a huge potential to boost its economy—what economists usually call the 'demographic dividend'. This is as opposed to a few decades ago, when India's population boom was described in menacing terms such as 'population explosion'.

Importantly, millennials and Generation Z have come of age at a time when online platforms and social media are available and offer them the ability and power to share opinions, influence people and question authority, seamlessly. These forces have had a strong role to play in shaping their world views, values and behaviours. From MeToo to Black Lives Matter and the convening of protest marches on climate change, these generations are compelling real change in society. The influence of these truly digital natives is only expanding. While young people have always embodied the spirit of their times, the influence of Gen Z—the first generation of true digital natives—has been enormous on account of these forces. As global connectivity soars, generational shifts could come to play a more important role in setting standards of social behaviour than economic forces have.

These seismic shifts also bring major implications for businesses, from both the consumer and employee perspective. Among other things, studies have found that newer generations place less value on work for its own sake and that the concept of work centrality has declined. According to Microsoft's Work Trend Index Annual Report, 51 per cent of Gen-Z employees are more likely to prioritize health and well-being over work. They also list 'positive culture' and a sense of purpose/meaning as their top priorities. Generally, they work to live versus live to work and they're drawn to employers who share their personal values.[3] LinkedIn's Workforce Confidence Report has found that as much as 80 per cent of Gen-Z employees are looking to work for companies whose values align with their own.[4]

Additionally, fostering a respectful, inclusive and diverse workplace culture is crucial to attracting and retaining top talent in today's competitive job market. According to a survey by Monster, as much as 83 per cent of Gen-Z candidates said a company's commitment to diversity and inclusion is important to them.[5]

Millennials and Gen Z also like to seek out employers who truly support their long-term career goals and ambitions. Companies that recognize this and provide a high level of support—from more time for skill development to imparting 'marketable' skills—are going to stay ahead in the war for talent.

Ironically, while Gen-Z employees are bringing their values and priorities to the workplace, research shows that

Gen Z is struggling with engagement at work. According to a 2022 Gallup Poll, 54 per cent of Gen-Z employees are ambivalent about work or not engaged at work.[6]

As such, it is essential for managers to understand what drives this generation, to support their Gen-Z employees and earn their full engagement.

How to engage Gen Z

Deloitte, in its report 'Welcome to Gen Z' notes that although money and salary are significant to Gen Z, other factors like work-life balance, flexible hours and perks and benefits are deeply valued because of the circumstances in which they grew up. In fact, in choosing between a higher-paying yet uninteresting job and a lower-paying but more engaging one, Gen Z appears to be equally divided. Of all the factors they value at work, flexibility and adaptability stand at the top.[7]

Similar trends were seen in a study by Fiverr (a popular online marketplace for freelancers), which collected answers from over 7000 Gen Z individuals around the world. The study showed that Gen Z prioritizes flexible, passion-driven work and entrepreneurship. As much as 40 per cent of the Zoomers (Gen Z) surveyed want to own a business or freelance throughout their career. Seventy-one per cent of the respondents said 'flexible working hours or the ability to be self-driven were top priorities when looking for a new job'. One-third of those surveyed reported that they work harder when working on something they are passionate about.[8]

Given the preferences for flexibility and greater agency among these generations, we may have to rely more on intrinsic motivation as opposed to external rewards when it comes to Gen Z.

In this context, the work of Edward L. Deci, a well-known professor of psychology at University of Rochester, on the negative effects external rewards can have on intrinsic motivation is worth examining. Specifically, if external rewards are seen as controlling or coercive, they can reduce a person's interest in the task in question and decrease their sense of autonomy. Deci conducted a series of experiments in which participants were given tasks to complete and were either offered rewards or not. He found that while rewards could initially increase performance, they also decreased intrinsic motivation in those who received them. Furthermore, when the rewards were removed, the decline in performance was sharper among the participants who had received rewards than among the participants who had never been offered any.[9]

Bestselling American author Daniel Pink has popularized these ideas, and his persuasive advice on founding motivation on the three pillars of autonomy, mastery and purpose fit in well with this generation.[10]

Coming to our core topic of the *future of work* and Gen Z, we can find an aha moment from watching among them the excellent interplay of technology and mindset. The flexibility that digital technologies enable in the design and delivery of work is exactly what Gen Z wants. In turn, the mindsets and preferences of Gen Z prepare them more than other generations to exploit fully the potential of technology-led *future of work*.

However, flexibility must go beyond tokenism and avoid mere band-aid solutions. The need of the hour is for managers to value the genuine blending of work and personal life and to look beyond 'presenteeism'. Interestingly, managers often forget that they too are employees.

The *future of work* can thrive only in futuristic cultures that foster experimentation and failure. The culture of the future must move away from authoritarian styles of the past, for they do not work when it comes to Gen-Z employees. The future generations of workers cannot be ordered around. They will flourish in a culture of mentorship and coaching. Young talent is eager to flex its entrepreneurial muscle. Allowing it to dream up and test bold ideas is clearly the way to go.

Additionally, organizations must ensure real-time communication between the young workforce and the top management. This is what a McKinsey report calls putting 'communication on steroids'.[11] Not only does the young workforce expect two-way communication, with inputs from everyone, but it also expects prompt action. It is also important to explain to these youth how their individual contributions matter and if they have made a difference at the workplace.

Gen Z and beyond: The India perspective

We must point out that in talking about Gen Z we have largely been referring to Western surveys and narratives. While some of these trends and needs are common among India's new youth, there are significant differences. Let me outline the top three that merit attention:

I.   **Family values:** India's Gen Z will continue to be embedded in India's unique family system, sharing deep bonds with parents and sometimes with members of the extended family. They will want independence, and yet, they will seek support and validation from their parents on crucial life choices. These strong values and bonds also tend to spill over into the workplace, where their relationships with managers are not purely contractual but also driven by the overall societal norms of tradition and respect.

II. **Obsession with formal education**: They will be more education oriented than their Western counterparts, especially rural Indians, who lay a lot of emphasis on getting formal degrees, certificates and academic credentials, and will go for the 'best and branded' colleges and the trending courses.

Career and fast growth orientation: Whether as formal employees or self-employed entrepreneurs, India's Gen Z is extraordinarily aspirational and somewhat restless. Their burgeoning aspirations to climb the socio-economic ladder, improve their lifestyles, access luxury goods, holiday abroad, etc., will dominate their work and life choices. In this matter, they are qualitatively different from their Western counterparts.

Therefore, while love of autonomy, purpose and flexibility will be common to Indian and Western Gen Z, the former's need for traditions, family bonds and fast growth will differentiate them from the latter.

Managers and leaders in India will be well advised to tailor their approaches to address these unique needs. Business leaders in India need to be particularly mindful about India's Gen Z being not driven merely by what their heart says, unlike many of their Western counterparts. Gen Z in India isn't just driven by what they want but also by what they think will be socially desirable. The fact that millions of Gen Z in India choose computer science and engineering degrees has a lot to do with the social desirability and implicit job promise associated with these choices (and not for the love of engineering). Driven by our unique cultural milieu, India's Gen Z will struggle over balancing security with freedom.

This career growth and social mobility orientation, coupled with India's unique traditions, must also inform how leaders in India must handle Gen Z's desire for independence and 'me space' on the one hand and a little intimacy and nurturing (as opposed to contractual) orientation on the other. This will be even more important in the case of youth from rural India, who are just about weaning away from family bonds and small-town camaraderie.

Truly, India's readiness for the *future of work* and its ability to integrate its rural youth into its workforce will critically depend on managers changing on two fronts: i) Replacing their command-control style of management with a more consultative style, and ii) Not adopting the often-common Western touch-me-not impersonal and contractual style.

Leaders in India must build a unique psychological contract with employees, which blends the old with the changing.

We must, in conclusion, point out that the *future of work* and Gen Z have a strong symbiotic relationship. Enabled by agile and collaborative technologies, the future of work will cater to the need for flexibility among the Gen Z. On the other hand, Gen Zs will shape the future of work by expecting work organizations to be more flexible. In the next chapter, we will investigate the detailed role different stakeholders can play in building future-ready organizations. What does it take to embrace the future and steer it to benefit all?

10

Building Flexible and Future-Ready Organizations

I cannot say whether things will get better if we change; what I can say is they must change if they are to get better.

—Georg C. Lichtenberg[1]

Most organizations continue to remain rooted in the industrial era, as we have discussed in several earlier chapters. Largely, the need for command-control, standardization and surveillance of work and workers continues to influence how we hire, pay, utilize and deal with workforces.

All of this, however, must be reset for the post-pandemic digital era. In times to come, workers across the world will demand greater freedom, flexibility and autonomy. Their ability to work virtually and remotely from anywhere will accentuate this demand.

What is the tone at the top?

While this transformation and reset must be driven from the top, our boards and CEOs continue to focus entirely on the here-and-now financial measures of success, often losing sight of the future. As boards pander to what Wall Street or Dalal Street expects of them, there is widespread, callous corporate social irresponsibility.

This current model of measuring firm success solely taking into account financial returns needs urgent change. The West created this model, with Wall Street, entrepreneurs, academics and consultants taking turns to defend a position famously known as the 'business of business is business'. This idea, first postulated by the noted economist Milton Friedman in 1970, refers to the classic capitalist focus on maximizing shareholder wealth, to the exclusion of other social responsibilities.[2] In fact, Western mainstream thinking is too deeply entrenched in this mindset, and therefore alternative and more balanced ideas like the B corp, or frameworks such as environmental, social and governance (ESG) face resistance even before they take off.

India need not follow this route. In fact, India's business doyens like J.R.D. Tata saw where the future lay and understood that business is not just about making money. We need to restore some of this spirit, especially given our vast inequities (reinforced by a divisive colonial past), and take a more balanced view of business. India is uniquely gifted to have visionaries like Gandhi, who could think of 'sarvodaya' even when serving long jail terms. Building on such ideas and blending them with the imperatives of a technology-driven *future of work*, we can build an India model of doing business that will help us leapfrog into developing economically, societally and culturally.

As we know from research, even in the most widely used definitions of corporate governance we do not see any reference to the people side of business.[3] Most constructs of corporate governance confine themselves to matters of resources, wealth creation and distribution. In India, the Uday Kotak report on corporate governance has made a significant contribution to the enhancement of corporate governance in the country.[4] The Kotak committee recommended several progressive steps to enhance the functioning of board committees, streamline the appointment of independent directors, improve disclosure requirements, etc. However, a close study of the recommendations, and especially those which have been accepted by SEBI, shows very little focus on people or employee aspects. Only three out of seventeen fully/ partially accepted recommendations deal with topics that demand HR expertise, viz: The Expanded role of the nomination and remuneration committee, the separation of chairman and CEO positions, requiring organization design and succession planning skills, and the appointment of at least one woman director, implying better and proactive sourcing of female talent. These are basics and reflect a 'let's-catch-up' mindset. Again, the opportunity to leapfrog and think ahead of the curve is being lost. While the burden of just getting the basics right is onerous, our opportunity is to pole vault and lead the pack. Our boards and CEOs must lead organizations into the future instead of reinventing their way through the experience of the so-called advanced nations. It is the paramount duty of boards and CEOs to unleash our country's vast human capital by building organizations that let people breathe and thrive.

It's high time boardroom discussions centred on questions such as:

- What does the *future of work* look like?
- What technologies will be appropriate in our context?
- How do we create jobs instead of killing them?
- How can we hire more inclusively, consciously including talented youth from rural India in our mix of 'diversity'?
- What are our investments in periodically upgrading and refreshing our internal systems, processes, structures and talent to stay fit for the future?
- How do we get our company to be an exciting place to work, where young people grow skilled and marketable, and get to unleash their full potential? How do we know this truly is happening, beyond the rhetoric, dashboards and occasional medals?
- How do we sustain people and talent investments into the uncertain future so neither the people nor the company are taken by a huge surprise?

What can CHROs do to build future-ready organizations?

Like many other aspects of organization management, HR systems and people management (by the way, the two are not the same—we must know that the HR function does not manage people, it is managers who manage people and the HR function builds systems for them). These systems need a complete upgrade to be ready for the future. CHROs must quickly rebuild several HR systems, like for hiring, induction, training, performance management, compensation, career development and exit management, factoring in the new imperatives of virtual and remote work. Additionally, with the changing demographics of the workforce, especially as Generation Z is set to be the bulk of the workforce, their needs also need to be factored in.

HR systems and people management approaches need to be rebuilt at two levels. First, we need to reset them for the post-pandemic work era, marked by employees demanding and exercising more choices. Second, the HR systems need to be adjusted for the new normal around WFH/WFA and, more broadly, any off-site remote work. Let's analyse these triggers of change more deeply, for they seem to be snowballing into tectonic shifts in how we design and apply HR systems in organizations.

Post-pandemic, some things about the employer-employee equation have permanently changed, at least in the more formal world of employment. 'We have changed. Work has changed. The way we think about time and space has changed,' says Tsedal Neeley, a professor at Harvard Business School and author of the book *Remote Work Revolution: Succeeding from Anywhere.*[5] I couldn't agree more.

The trauma of the pandemic and the opportunity of 'working from anywhere' have been the twin forces bringing about a fundamental transformation in the world of work.

Paul Krugman puts it succinctly in an incisive *New York Times* article:

When something—like, say, a deadly pandemic—forces them out of their rut, they realize what they've been putting up with. And because they can learn from the experience of other workers, there may be a 'quits multiplier' in which the decision of some workers to quit ends up inducing other workers to follow suit.[6]

In India too, where we have much less social and financial security, twenty-somethings today are much choosier about what they want to do and whom they want to work for.

The writing on the wall is clear: We need to question the assumptions of motivation and engagement on which the pre-pandemic HR systems (largely a hangover from the early industrial era) were built.

The best way to break away from the inertia of the status quo is to take a leap of faith and embrace new practices. Since this book is not designed to provide cookbook-style solutions, I will refrain from recommending specific HR practices. What I aim to do instead is to give enough ideas to munch on and stimulate out-of-the-box thinking. Here, therefore, are a few high-level ideas for key HR processes in the post-pandemic era.

Employer branding: This should ideally be the starting point for any company's people journey. It begs the question of why people should work for you. As you answer this question, you begin to define your employee value proposition. Traditionally, you did this by assembling a few top people and crafted a cool statement about the great stuff for which you wanted to be known.

A brand, however, is not what you say it is, but is what others experience you as. This practice, therefore, doesn't work, especially when employees will check you out using GlassDoor or other similar apps. Instead of you deciding what the company wants to be known for, it is for candidates, employees, ex-employees, interns and other stakeholders to decide what you are already known for. You will be authentic, honest and differentiated only if your brand communicates your true self.

Sourcing: After you have defined an authentic employee value proposition, you will now actively look at sourcing candidates who will be eager to work for you. The biggest new opportunity that the post-pandemic times offer you lies beyond the traditional talent pools, where you can now look. With flexible work options, enabled in part by technology and in part by the change in employer attitudes, you can now reach out to a whole range of new talent that was earlier excluded. Homemakers, people with different abilities, minorities and, most importantly, rural folk, will be the new catchment groups. Additionally, with a 100-year lifespan staring at us, we can now even reach people in their seventies, for example, and tap into their experience and maturity.[7]

In India, sourcing has been traditionally skewed towards the English-proficient, urban male graduates from elite colleges who are often engineers. This is only a small section of our vast talent pool. Sadik and Brown (2020) examined the recruitment practices of thirteen leading corporations in high-growth sectors in India.[8] Based on detailed qualitative interviews, they explain why 'these corporations are unlikely to increase the demand for graduates in ways imagined by policymakers or proponents of skills-biased technological change. Companies in India are locked into an intense "war for talent", but only with the graduates in India's top-tier universities'. The interesting implication is that Indian companies are biased towards elite schools. Yes, some talent from elite schools needs to be hired for certain job types. But over-reliance on pedigree is neither business friendly nor nation friendly.

It's time to rise above such narrow considerations and actively look for rural, vernacular-educated men, and more importantly women, who are skilled more than educated. This shift will be further enabled by the remote and flexible work options that the post-pandemic era allows us to embrace. It is about time that we thought of democratizing access to jobs instead of selectively reaching out to a privileged few.

In fact, we have something interesting to learn from what the Indian IT major TCS is getting done through TCS iON, its strategic unit for building cloud-based solutions for manufacturing and education. It is democratizing recruitment by giving all candidates access to a single, standardized, high-quality benchmark test to showcase their competency to top recruiters, while at the same time making this pre-certified talent pool available for corporations to hire.[9] Such transparent and accessible pathways are also being provided by many others, including government arms. We need to double down on these and expand their reach. By changing our conventional and default thinking around sourcing, we will not only mitigate the challenges of talent shortages but also unleash the vast human capital of India.

The other major re-think needs to be around the preference for those 'who-have-been-there-and-done-that'. In fact, future jobs will in no way be like the ones of the past. We clearly need to source and hire for future-ready skills and not for length of experience or parity with incumbent job titles. This skills-first approach will mark much of future hiring, as a recent LinkedIn research suggests.[10] As explained in this report, the big shift in the future will be to assess candidates based on their skills and learning and not on their degrees, qualifications and job titles. Based on their study, LinkedIn reported: 'In the last year, more than 45% of hirers on LinkedIn explicitly used skills data to fill their roles, up 12% year over year. Roughly one in five job postings (19%) in the US no longer requires degrees, up from 15% in 2021.'

Interviewing: It's about time we changed the power equation between employers and employees. Employers need to stop acting like gods that dole out jobs in return for subservience. Have you ever thought why employers alone should interview candidates and not the other way around? Today an employer can formally do a reference check, background checks and probe into every aspect of a prospective employee. What if we provided the same facilities to candidates to review, assess and interview employers before deciding the 'fit' between their capabilities and aspirations and what the employer has to offer? Taking this argument further, what if 'employers' are put on a 'trial period' (something like the probation employees are put through), during which candidates can 'try' out a company and decide if it will be mutually suitable for them to continue there?

Post-pandemic, many people have started questioning employment as we understand it traditionally. People want to gig it out, knowing how important it is to live than merely slog away. Under these circumstances, employers will be lucky if people are willing to consider working for them. As an employer, knowing this early and offering your best to be selected by discerning employees will be a great and welcome reversal of roles between employers and employees.

Overall, it's time to rehaul the long, one-sided interview process and turn it on its head—to officially recognize the importance of employees choosing employers.

Induction: Through the last several decades, induction has degenerated into 'indoctrination' in most companies. A typical induction programme for new employees runs like this: The new guys are taken in a bunch into a conference room; they are given company T-shirts and shown company videos, including a recorded message of the CEO welcoming them and telling them how great the company is. No new joiner gives a damn about this, but the charade goes on. It's time we took a relook at this farce and did something fundamentally different. Let the new employees 'discover' the company through structured floor walks, site visits, meets, projects, document reviews, interviews with key personnel; let them meet customers and other stakeholders, understand the financials and governance aspects and analyse for themselves what they see. Let them debrief you after their discovery and inquiry. This will keep you on your toes as an employer and also make them accountable in finding their place in the organization instead of being spoon-fed.

Training: More often termed learning and development, training should be about improving marketable skills and not consist of 'remedial' or mere proprietary education in non-transferable skills. Quite a few companies are still stuck in the old assumptions that training is a great expense and that it should not be wasted on employees who will not pledge their loyalty to the company. Think about it: New-gen employees do not work for you to retire with you. They work so that their resumes improve and their market value goes up. If they do not 'grow' through market-relevant training and value-adding experiences, they will move to other shores where that is possible. The more you train and grow them, the more they are likely to stick with you.

Performance management: Think of it honestly: What HR folks refer to as a performance management system (PMS) is largely a process that requires managers to fill out a set of forms and templates, increasingly online, and rate or assess their employees, eventually with a view to ranking them as great, good and not-so-good employees. This, in turn, is used to give the employees 'increments' or merit increases, usually annually. This is hardly about performance management. This is a templated attempt to differentiate between employees to decide who should get what increment, and not a very successful one at that.

A whiff of fresh air came when Deloitte, one of the world's largest professional services firms, made headlines in 2015 when it announced its decision to completely reinvent its performance management system.[11] The company found that its previous system, which relied on annual performance reviews and rankings, was too time-consuming, demotivating for employees and didn't accurately reflect their performance.

Deloitte reinvented its performance management system by moving away from its traditional approach of annual 360-degree feedback and implementing a more agile and real-time system. The new approach includes regular check-ins and ongoing feedback between managers and employees, as well as the setting of goals that are tailored to individual employee strengths and career aspirations.

This new approach is designed to increase employee engagement, promote ongoing development and improve overall performance. It also emphasizes the importance of coaching and mentoring, and places a greater emphasis on individual accountability for professional growth and development.

Unfortunately, these new directions are still very much confined to a few progressive firms. The bulk of companies across the world are still struggling with performance appraisal, not to speak of performance management. Most

PMSes are still just the boss's opinion on subordinates and are largely used for either remedial or reward actions. One *Washington Post* business writer called it a *'rite of corporate kabuki'*, which restricts creativity, generates mountains of paperwork and serves no real purpose.[12]

We have a long way to go in rethinking and redesigning performance management systems. But the fundamental switch has to be about making it an employee-owned and initiated action (as opposed to an HR-owned chasing action). Imagine a situation where, periodically, employees shed their current reluctance and voluntarily go to their managers and say: 'This is the evidence of what I contributed to the company, what do you think I should do, more or differently, to make our company great and successful?'

With work-model changes consequent to wider adoption of work-from-any-where type of virtual work formats, conventional effort-centred measures and goals will not work any more. Since managers cannot, and perhaps should not, *oversee* what employees do in real time, we need to agree on outcomes and let employees take stock of how they are doing on agreed outcomes, periodically. Moving from effort measures to outcome measures, however, needs a serious mindset change. Managers need to trust their employees—an important prerequisite for remote work to succeed.[13]

So much for how PMS needs to be redesigned. Managers need to change too, to use such an enhanced system, which we will discuss shortly.

Compensation and total rewards: The new era also calls for an urgent review of centuries-old beliefs about how people must be paid and incentivized for the jobs they do. I propose four distinct factors that must inform HR leaders and policymakers as they redesign compensation for the new India: 1. The big picture of growing income inequalities, 2. The whole phenomenon of subsistence wages in the informal unorganized sector, 3. The belief that incentives work, and 4. The top-down approaches of doling out wages instead of a participatory process of earning income for one's contributions.

Firm- or organization-level compensation must be revisited in the larger context of the stark socio-economic inequities in the world. Let's see the big picture first. Today, the world's richest 1 per cent owns nearly twice as much wealth as the rest of the world put together.[14]

In the US, chief executives at S&P 500 companies made 324 times more than the median worker at their companies in 2021, according to an annual report from the largest labour union federation in the US, AFL-CIO.[15]

In India too there is a huge chasm between CXO salaries and other employee salaries. A recent *Business Standard* analysis revealed that a typical Indian CEO's salary in FY21 was 184x the median employee salary. The ratio was up from 174x in FY20 and 179x in FY19.[16]

We cannot build an equitable society unless these excesses are addressed.

It is time policymakers and corporate leaders owned this challenge and voluntarily restricted and imposed ceilings on such vast pay differentials.

While steep wage gaps are a problem on the one hand, the low wages earned by the vast majority of Indians lie at the other end of the problem. We must urgently address the wage adequacy challenge. While the available data is questionable and varies vastly, depending whom you ask, it can be safely said that more than 70 per cent of Indians are in informal jobs that do not fetch them decent wages. Far from the aspirational living wages, India's vast majority is paid mere subsistence wages. Even within the relatively formalized sector of the small and micro-enterprises (bulk providers of non-farm jobs), wages hover at minimum levels. This dismal picture is not consistent with India's aspirations of becoming a $5-trillion economy and of finally featuring among the top three economies of the world. Most economists agree that productivity is the key to better wages. Productivity, in turn, is a factor of many forces, like deployable and proven knowledge and skills (human capital), efficient work systems, supportive administrative and legal systems, optimal use of fit-for-purpose enabling technologies and a strong work culture. India does not have the luxury of allowing organic evolution and maturing of all these factors. Trying to find macro- and national-level solutions could lead to boiling the ocean. Instead, we must work urgently on improving this situation through several micro-actions.

The question to ask is, what can individual firms—mega, big, medium, small, micro and start-ups—do to substantially (if not fully) address this poor wage issue? Here is the proposition: If, as an employer, I can believe that by paying 'good and decent' wages I can attract and deploy skilled employees and gain in productivity, I can create a virtuous cycle of decent wages leading to higher productivity leading to larger economic surpluses, which in turn will support decent wages. Most entrepreneurs have an ad-hoc and opportunistic compensation philosophy and refuse to commit to a longer-term and sustainable wage regimen. The root cause lies in the treatment of wages as 'expenses' and not investment. But if mindsets change and each CEO and entrepreneur can take micro-actions at their units, their progressive actions, eventually, can be a large force for good for the whole of society, paving the path for unleashing India's vast human capital.

In the post-pandemic world, the poor-wages issue has gained a new significance. We can now move city-based jobs to small towns and pay decent wages to the rural folk. Imagine the same software engineer getting her Bengaluru salary in Hubbali or Horanadu. With people earning urban salaries in rural towns, several knock-on benefits will occur, not just for employees like this engineer but for the entire town. Local spending will increase, leading to tertiary employment. Tell-tale urban symbols, like pizza outlets, coffee bars, salons and gyms, will pop up in these small towns, which will have multiplier effects on the local economy. If the much celebrated UPI and India stack are creating financial inclusion, moving decent jobs to small towns will create human capital inclusion.

Incentives or bribes: The unquestioned belief that incentives always work is one of the side effects of the predominant shareholder-centricity of contemporary corporations, reinforced by Wall Street pundits and their academic and consulting partners. Of course, in the same West, where the business of business became the only business, a fair amount of thinking is happening around the detrimental short-termism that such an approach breeds.

Let's first understand the origins of incentives. It all started with the behaviourists. Through experiments on animals, it was asserted that we all respond positively to rewards/incentives and negatively to punishments. Researchers have demonstrated how accidental connections between ritual and favourable consequences can establish and maintain behaviours.[17] This simplified view of human behaviour got translated into corporate 'incentive' programmes, initially at Ford, GE and other such large organizations, and eventually spreading across the world. Explaining why incentive plans cannot work brilliantly, Alfie Kohn in his book *Punished by Rewards* makes an important observation: '*What we use bribes to accomplish may have changed, but the reliance on bribes, on behaviorist doctrine, has not.*'[18] In essence, rewards are bribes—the former legitimized by select academics, consultants and corporate practitioners acting in concert; and the latter criticized by a section of helpless citizens who are adversely impacted by them. But there is abundant evidence that financial incentives do not work as we assume they do. We will discuss this more as we analyse what motivates people.

But here is the problem. While there is huge evidence that incentives do not work, the Wall Street-led model and the measure of quarterly corporate success have built a strong 'received wisdom' around incentives and pay-for-performance plans that ordinary managers find hard to challenge.

Now let's turn our attention to the twin forces of digitalization and demographic shifts in emerging economies coinciding with lingering fears about pandemics and climate disruptions. Aided by these, the *future of work* will be marked by two distinct shifts: i) More and more work will be done on digital platforms, which lend to modularization of work like never before. This time it is knowledge work that will be 'piece-rated'. And the key difference between piece-rating manufacturing and knowledge work is that while you can produce more standardized 'pins' within the same hour if paid more, you cannot perhaps produce more algorithms of any significance just because you are paid more. In this new world of increased cognitive work, mindless replication of industrial-era incentives will backfire. ii) The emergence of Gen Z and Gen Alpha as the predominant members of the workforce all over the world, including in India. They will not choose to slave for a little more money. These new generations will value 'experience' over 'earnings' and push for purpose over profits. These two forces will compel us to revisit our entrenched assumptions around incentives.

It is time we stopped overrating incentives and bonuses and be circumspect about their mass deployment.

What should managers do differently?

In most organizations, there are managers in between the invisible employer and the employees, and it is their existence that is most challenged. I love the way Janan Ganesh, one of my favourite columnists in the *Financial Times,* says, 'There is grandeur in ownership. There is dignity in labour. It's the tier between that has to plead for its reputation.'[19]

This reputation is under greater threat now, when Gen Z, armed with *future of work* tools, is questioning the need for managers. Here are two ways in which managers can change and be future ready.

First, managers must reimagine their roles—from being instructors and reviewers to coaches and resource persons. A lot is being written and spoken about all this in the present times, but nothing much has changed on the ground. The hangover of the industrial-era hierarchy is huge and heavy. What best organizations are able to do is to tinker with the system and introduce new tactical practices, like 'check-ins', to habituate managers to frequently engage with employees. While all these practices are done with good intentions, they will not deliver fundamental and enduring change unless the imperatives of an employee-centred approach are fully understood and internalized.

Second, the overall transition from 'appraisal' to management of performance needs to be undertaken, which requires three fundamental shifts: i) A move from top-down goal setting to co-creation of outcomes-based measures, ii) Belief in and practice of feedback as a gift (we may say about feedback what Portia had said about mercy in the memorable Shakespearean play *Merchant of Venice*: 'It is twice blest: It blesseth him that gives and him that takes', and iii) A new-age PMS that will help people improve their performance rather than merely find out who is not performing. Such key shifts require investment in mindsets and belief systems first, while tactics and practices can follow.

How to engage with employees better

It's a pity that employee engagement often degenerates into employee entertainment. Friday parties, birthday celebrations, fun events and off-site retreats are often termed as engagement activities, while in reality they merely entertain employees, that too transiently. Little surprise, then, that a survey on employee engagement by Gallup, a global analytics and advice firm, reveals that as of 2022, only 32 per cent of full- and part-time employees working for US organizations were engaged, while 18 per cent were actively disengaged at the workplace.[20] The India numbers, as per a survey conducted by Leena AI, an innovative technology solutions platform, were 23 per cent for employees not actively engaged at the workplace.[21]

The reasons for the failure to create engagement among a vast majority of the workforce across company types are many. But let me call out the underlying confusion, especially in the context of India. Most managers do not look for the precise meaning of engagement. As we know, engagement is best measured as the willingness on the part of employees to put in discretionary effort in the interest of the company. Take the example of employees of Taj Hotels giving up their lives to save customers and face terrorist bullets bravely. This is an extreme example of deep engagement with a company besides the beliefs and value systems of these individuals. While we do not ordinarily expect employees to sacrifice their lives for the company, this example reminds us how employees give their best and go beyond the call of duty when fully engaged.

The next major misunderstanding among managers is the belief that any or all three of these factors: i) Feel good, ii) Welfare, and iii) Loyalty lead to engagement. Most engagement programmes are based on these beliefs. True engagement, however, happens when employees experience their managers as genuinely invested in their growth and development. Employees feel engaged when they see meaning in their work, when they feel their ideas are valued, or at least heard, when they can contribute to and participate in the company, when their learning leads to growth in skills and competencies and when they see their 'marketability' growing due to the significant experiences they are getting in their current job. Doing all the above means hard work, homework and the honing of one's managerial skills. These are very different from the fun-based offerings we often make in the name of engagement. Behind the glitz and glamour of modern offices, managers are still evolving into their true role of stewardship. Enduring engagement cannot be delivered until managers shed their old habits of command and control. To be relevant into the future, they need to grow into being performance enablers and career coaches, and to facilitate meaning and decode their purpose at work, thus making work less of drudgery.

Managers in the virtual world

While we have discussed the unmet needs of brick-and-mortar workspaces, a whole new order of virtual work arrangements have emerged post-pandemic. We are likely to settle into a world of work that will have a large component of fully or partially remote work and/or hybrid work. Generating engagement in this new remote world, where the familiar physical location and the touch and feel of office are missing, is an entirely new challenge. This is a fundamental shift, for which there is no parallel in human history. There can, therefore, be no universal prescriptions or established theories to explain the emergent challenges. But we do have some solid hypotheses and some partially tested propositions about how managers might create engagement in the new virtual world of work. My own research with close to 1500 IT and pharma-sector employees in India presented three actionable insights:[22] i) Managers need to be deliberately inclusive and cold-call employees while on virtual mode to signal: 'I care'. ii) Managers need to set up one-on-one video calls with their employees, not to 'check-in' and convert every encounter into a performance discussion but to have adult-like heart-to-heart conversation, to listen with a view to hearing out the employees and empathize with them, and iii) Managers must trust unconditionally and create 'swift trust'.[23]

Our collective experience in managing virtual work will only grow. For now, a good starting point is to understand that presence is no proxy for productivity. Not all the people who are working off-site are cheating. The benefits of giving people the flexibility of doing their work from anywhere far outweigh the risks.[24]

How to motivate the workforce of the future

In more recent times, Daniel Pink, an American author who is also known as a television host as well as speechwriter for former vice president Al Gore, has challenged the conventional wisdom, arguing that while money remains the hygiene, real motivation comes from autonomy, mastery and purpose. In his book *Drive,* he asserts that the secret to high performance and satisfaction—at work, at school and at home—is the deeply human need to direct our own lives, to learn and create new things, and to do better by ourselves and our world.[25] In his book, he refers to a research conducted in 2002 in the Indian town of Madurai, Tamil Nadu, where Dan Ariely and a group of researchers went to Madurai, to test the effects of incentives on performance. They asked eighty-seven individuals to play a series of games, ranging from tossing tennis balls at a target to recalling a sequence of digits. All the tasks utilized motor skills, creativity or concentration. The researchers divided the participants into three groups. The first group was offered a small reward of Rs 4 to complete the tasks. The second group was given a larger incentive of Rs 40. The third group was offered the highest reward of Rs 400. The results indicated that increased incentives worsened performance. The Rs-40 group performed no better than the Rs-4 group, and the Rs-400 individuals performed substantially worse than those in the other two groups by every measure. 'In eight of the nine tasks we examined across the three experiments, higher incentives led to worse performance.'[26]

Much earlier, in 1971, Edward L. Deci, a well-known professor of psychology at University of Rochester, proposed, based on his research, that external rewards can have negative effects on intrinsic motivation. Specifically, if external rewards are seen as controlling or coercive, they can reduce people's interest in a task and decrease their sense of autonomy. Deci conducted a series of experiments in which participants were given tasks to complete and were either offered rewards or not. He found that while rewards could initially increase performance, they also decreased intrinsic motivation among the recipients. Furthermore, when the rewards were removed, the rewarded participants' performance declined even further than the performance of participants who had never been offered rewards.

In the post-pandemic world, intrinsic motivation resonates strongly, especially with Gen Z. The well-known consulting company Deloitte, in its report 'Welcome to Gen Z', notes that although money and salary are significant to Gen Z, due to the circumstances in which they grew up, other factors also hold importance. These include work-life balance, flexible hours, and perks and benefits, which Gen Z feels entitled to from employers, in addition to salary. In fact, when presented with the choice of a higher-paying yet uninteresting job or a lower-paying but more engaging one, Gen Z appears to be equally divided between the two.

In summary, it is time our simplistic notions of what motivates people are revisited. The future generations will demand more autonomy, purpose and mastery from their work. Indian organizations have two options: Either they can go through the same painful realization that the West is going through and be the last movers to building organizations of the future; or they can catapult themselves, ushering in new, people-friendly organizations by embracing the *future of work* more imaginatively.

India's largest capital is its human capital. It will be in our collective interest to build such new-age organizations, not only in Mumbai but also in Munnar.

11

Is Flexibility Feasible? Points and Counterpoints

A way of seeing is also a way of not seeing.

—Kenneth Burke[1]

Even as the twin forces of the pandemic and digitalization have paved the path towards more flexible forms of work, there has been a strong employer-employee divide on what is feasible. Now that fears about the pandemic have subsided, many employers want their employees to return to office. The accommodations they showed during the pandemic have been withdrawn. Three years after the deadly virus attack, we are largely unsure about how we should shape the *future of work*. We refuse to rethink work delivery models and work contracts. Many of the ideas we have discussed in the earlier chapters sound desirable to some but utopian to others. Since there are many ways of seeing this evolving phenomenon, it will be useful to examine the most common objections to the new forms of flexibility and also present the possible counter-arguments to them—in the spirit of gaining perspective, staying open and not being dogmatic about anything. In this chapter, I will argue for both sides and present the points and counterpoints around the feasibility of work flexibility. While there are many views and opinions on how flexible we can be with work and the workforce, here are the top *five* concerns that we must address. There can be many more, but these five have often bothered me and have been thrown at me as I teach the *future of work* to MBAs or advise executives.

All jobs cannot be done remotely. If we let some jobs (IT) stay remote, we will be creating a new caste system.

Point

It is true that currently all jobs cannot be done remotely. People still must go to factories, retail stores, hospitals, horticultural farms and restaurants to work. IT and white-collar jobs have lent themselves to remote working easily due to the very nature of the work involved. In fact, the idea of employees working away from the office and from a place of their choice (earlier termed 'telecommuting') has always raised eyebrows. Those who worked in smokestack factories saw the rise of IT workers with envy and felt what today's idiom terms as FOMO (fear of missing out). Further, among office workers, permission to work from home was always granted as a special privilege and accommodation for workers with special needs. Therefore, a shift to mass-scale work from non-office locations, almost as a default, is indeed seen as licence and not freedom. The objections are natural, human and valid. On top of it, we have not had an easy way to classify jobs as 'remote-able' or otherwise.

While media stories on how drones are spraying pesticides and delivering medicines in farms and villages, or how robots are running factories and warehouses, are read with interest, they look far-fetched. The lived experiences of millions of Indians still consist of pushing wheelbarrows along crowded streets on a mid-summer morning or climbing twenty floors over makeshift scaffolding with a basket of bricks on their heads. Overall, the discussion on work taking different shapes sounds unrealistic, academic and unfeasible to many. Under these circumstances, it may be appropriate to consider, at this time, that all jobs cannot be remote, and if some can be, they will be seen with unease, leading to feelings among those in other jobs of losing out, if not of being blatantly discriminated against. For some time more in India, remote work will be seen as a 'privilege' and will feel like it is creating a new caste system.

Counterpoint

This point leads to three other subpoints like: (i) I know many jobs can be done remotely, and when that happens and I can benefit from it, I will cease to see it as discrimination, and until then I will remain concerned and call it a 'caste system' (ii) I sense that by going remote I am a victim of the 'out of sight, out of mind' syndrome. I feel I will be penalized for working from home, and hence my question is more about discrimination and less about what jobs can be done remotely, and (iii) I don't want to be classified as remote or on-site. I want to choose the options that best work for me at various points in time. If such flexibility is not provided, I will remain concerned about any classification.

I have often found these underlying opinions among all those who have questions about remote work. I decode the problem as lack of visibility, flexibility, and the opportunity to have a say. All systems look rigid if people can't have a say in them.

Employers and the so-called thought leaders have confined themselves to a rather narrow narrative that frames the issue as home vs office. The pandemic has opened the proverbial Pandora's box around 'flexibility'.

I understand flexibility can't be a one-way street. If work needs to be done, we must have some guardrails and a strong code of conduct. For us in India, this issue may get resolved quicker than imagined, for we have been used to complete inflexibility for a long time and any small dose of flexibility will bring in the much-needed relief for all. We need to frame the issue of the rise of flexibility as a condition for productive and engaged work. More importantly, when such flexibility informs our employment and work models, we will be able to include many more of our talented people waiting outside the gates of formal employment.

When everyone has equal opportunities, employment will be less discriminatory, and factory workers will join the party as soon as technology enables them to. How we work has always depended on the nature of our work. People from different occupations will have different realities to contend with—until technology provides all a level playing field. In the interim, arguments that say flexible work promotes a new caste system are, naturally, expected explanations for our resistance to change and are not fundamentally about the question of discrimination.

There is a huge digital divide in India. Our rural folk cannot participate in remote work.

Point

This is a serious issue. During the pandemic, we heard horror stories of depression and suicide among young students who could not complete their homework since the father took away the only smartphone available to the family.

According to a report by the Internet and Mobile Association of India (IAMAI) and Nielsen, as of November 2021, Internet users in rural India accounted for 38 per cent of the total Internet user base in the country, whereas urban India accounted for 62 per cent of the total Internet user base.[2]

The situation gets worse when we add the gender dimension. Women in India are less likely to have Internet access than men. As of November 2021, average Internet penetration among women in India was 23 per cent, against 43 per cent among men. Access to the Internet, tablets, smartphones and other work-enabling devices is both low and unevenly spread in India.[3] This does pose a challenge in taking serious work to rural India.

Counterpoint

This is a chicken-and-egg situation. Just a little before the pandemic, most Indians were very critical about the availability of reliable mobile and Internet services. But through the pandemic and now, millions of Indians have moved to video calling, and large parts of business and work do get done online routinely. In the 1980s, when

Indians were trusted by US and European clients to deliver IT work remotely, we had limited and unreliable Internet infrastructure. But the cost arbitrage opportunity made our friends from the advanced countries take a leap of faith and give us work. We caught up with technology and delivered. If we do the same with our country folk, they too will rise. India has an ambitious plan to provide broadband Internet connectivity to all. The BharatNet programme, which aims to provide high-speed broadband connectivity to all gram panchayats in the country, is one of the key initiatives for promoting digital connectivity and digital empowerment in rural India. As of November 2021, it appears we have already covered 50 per cent of our gram panchayats with optical fibre networks. We must take a leap of faith here and start offering urban jobs in rural areas. That will create demand for better Internet services, which in turn will support more jobs, thus creating a virtuous cycle. The only way to address the digital divide is to take it head on.

Many people live in small, congested homes, with demanding caregiving responsibilities. Offices provide them with a better work environment.

Point

This truly is an India-specific challenge. This confirms our view that all *future of work* possibilities do not immediately apply in India and other such crowded and low per-capita-income countries. In my research engagements with Indian companies, I have come across several interesting insights as to why young Indians, and especially women, want to go to the office. The insights from women are particularly revealing and compel us to avoid offering easy solutions.

Many women told me (and we all know this) that they find the office a necessary escape from the tyranny of their 'in-laws' and the associated pressures of 'serving them' when at home. India's cultural norm of expecting women to provide additional caregiving, and sometimes show sheer subservience, to the elder members of the joint family have not changed. Truly, for women, the office is a great relief from this domestic tyranny. Similarly, for bachelors living in low-cost rented apartments in the big cities, every day is a daily survival struggle. Compared with their ill-equipped dorms, modern offices are a luxury indeed. It's not uncommon to find a typical bachelor, usually a male in his late twenties, come in early to office, use the on-premise gym and the shower rooms, get breakfast in the company cafeteria, help himself to the free tea/coffee and beverages at the office through the day, hang out with colleagues/friends for evening snacks, play pool and other indoor games in the office, have dinner at the office food court and go back to his dorm only to sleep.

Crowded homes, gender-unequal sociocultural norms and plush offices will continue to make many choose office over home for work.

Counterpoint

Let us look at this carefully. The preference for the office, in this argument, is not as a place to work but as a place to eat, play, socialize and escape to. This fact, when understood fully, clears many cobwebs around offices as places for productive work. I guess for some time we need to continue offices as they provide shelter, as it were, to some employees. But over time, two shifts will usher in a new paradigm. The first—that with rising incomes and infrastructure, dorms and single accommodations will evolve to become more comfortable as they already are in the big cities. Small towns will catch up if there is employment. For families in the big cities, builders are already offering 'two bedrooms plus home office' kind of accommodation. This trend will rise, given the pain of commuting and the rising affordability of home offices and/or colocation workspaces for India's formal sector workers. Secondly, if urban jobs move to rural towns, people will fall back on families and protective communities and will not trade off the emotional comfort of family for the impersonal benefits of the office. This is the reason why many who have gone back to their hometowns are unwilling to return to their place of work in the big cities.

Of course, sociocultural norms must change, both in cities and small towns, and men must become equal partners in domestic chores. This will take time. We are seeing green shoots of mindset change and behaviours and the sheer necessity of double income in the family, which will make men relent and own up to their part of the responsibilities at home.

I envision that homes and staycations will soon be the new offices. And offices will be the new hang-out places for fun, socializing and camaraderie.

Remote work has led to an increase in moonlighting. Managers will find it hard to control remote workers.

Point

This is an important concern. It is true that several employees have misused their new-found freedom (think of how most employees turn off their cameras while on video calls). Many are found absenting, non-responsive and absconding, in sheer breach of the employment contract. The recent controversy in India over 'moonlighting' is a collective protest against abuse of work by employees, and rightly so. Many employers have installed surveillance tools on their employee's laptops to keep a watch on them. IT major Wipro had to fire 300 employees in 2022 for moonlighting.[4]

Counterpoint

Moonlighting is not a new phenomenon. Remote working could have given it a fillip, but even from within the confines of their offices some people have always done side hustles. Think of employees doing day trading from the comfort of their office desks. Having them in office in person has not been able to stop such unacceptable behaviours.

Future employees can't be managed through surveillance. Given the importance of autonomy and agency, they will need less supervision and micro-management. In fact, there is a ton of research that tells us how self-managed teams outperform micro-managed teams.[5] Rini van Solingen, a tenured professor at the Delft University of Technology in the Netherlands, offers an interesting perspective on this by comparing two types of management—shepherding and beekeeping.[6] He talks about how, if you want to develop self-managing teams, you need to stop treating your people like sheep. A shepherd, much like a traditional manager, tells the sheep exactly which direction to follow, what to eat, where to eat, and checks on them to see that everything is the way he wants it to be. This is the typical command-and-control pattern of management. The shepherd even gets himself a dog, which listens to his commands and barks to the sheep to steer them in the right direction. Beekeeping, on the other hand, is fundamentally different from shepherding. Bees work on their own, and the better the environment the more honey they produce. When bees do not produce the expected amount of honey, the beekeeper looks at the environment and works to improve it. So too should managers look at their environment. The key to developing self-managing teams is to trust employees to deliver their best. Clearly, then, the first step is for managers to change themselves from shepherds to beekeepers.

As we measure performance through outcomes, monitoring of efforts requiring in-person oversight will gain less significance. As we trust more, teams will reciprocate. As we invest in skills and competencies, employees will need less handholding.

For centuries, our only way of monitoring work was to have the worker literally under our noses. In India, 'presenteeism' (the tendency to be present in the office irrespective of how you are feeling) has gone to great lengths. Traditionally, in many of our workplaces, the owner/boss has the right to expect the employee to be at his 'disposal'. Many employees make it a point to hang on in the office, usually within visible range of the big boss till the boss leaves the office, so that the boss notices his 'hard work'. Over centuries, in-person proximity has been a synonym for work and productivity. No wonder managers lack the skills to manage and oversee virtual teams.

India, like many other former colonies of the once mighty British empire, has the additional challenge of having to free itself from its feudal mindset and learn to not consider leadership as bossing over someone. We must adopt 'unbossing', as Lars Kolind and Jacob Bøtter advocate in their book *Unboss*. 'The Unboss is more servant than master. The unboss is somebody who makes things possible instead of issuing orders. A leader rather than a boss. A designer rather than a producer.'[7] We must hurry in this direction before our youth decides to abandon formal employment altogether. And we must remember that when we had everyone under our noses there was no less cheating (!).

When employees work remotely, building collaboration and a strong company culture is hard.

Point

Among the various objections to flexible and remote working options, the most serious is the issue of culture. Based on what we know as academics and practitioners, cultures always got built and maintained through in-person interactions or communities. Reed Hastings, CEO of Netflix, was rightly anxious when he said, 'Culture isn't just something you can create in a vacuum. It's about the daily interactions, the shared experiences and the spontaneous moments of collaboration that happen when people are physically together. That's much harder to achieve when everyone is working from home.' He is not alone. Many celebrity CEOs have voiced their opinion against employees working from home, among other reasons, for diluting the company culture. In India too, Azim Premji, the well-known CEO of WIPRO, the IT major, expressed concerns about remote work, stating that 'the culture of the organization is impacted adversely by the lack of in-person interactions'.

With remote work, normal culture building activities, like company events, training, leadership role modelling, mentoring, etc., have become difficult. Observing colleagues and senior leaders at work has been our default mode of soaking in and imbibing the culture of the company. It is true, as the corporate folklore of yesteryear demonstrates, that many youngsters who joined as management trainees grow over the years to become the CEOs of the same companies, imbibing and in turn role-modelling the culture of the company. Big Indian companies—Tata, Reliance, Birla, Mahindra, ITC, L&T, Infosys, etc.—have conventionally believed in their own home-grown cultures, which have been ingrained in their people over the years.

Given such deeply entrenched experiences and beliefs among leaders, it's no wonder that people not coming together every day to the workplace is bothering a lot of them. They are largely clueless about how to build a culture in the increasingly virtual world.

Counterpoint

It would be some time before we can figure out how to build culture in the virtual work world. But, to look at it differently, one notices that while the classic model of leaders defining culture and others imbibing it in the in-person world is being challenged, the virtual world has already built its own culture. Between 'influencers' and viral videos on Instagram, or X, we are already witnessing powerful new mechanisms by which culture spreads, which perhaps the in-person world could not achieve. Going forward, we must ponder upon whether culture should result from a-few-deciding-and-others-following type of top-down corporate initiative, or from crowd-sourced co-creation of shared beliefs and actions transmitted through real-time digital media, with parallel engagement on the part of all stakeholders. Yes, we had one type of culture, both as an outcome and as a process. But there is reason to believe that with the virtual world settling down, both what we mean by culture and how we build it may undergo fundamental shifts.

Interestingly, a study by researchers at the World Economic Forum found that 'remote and hybrid working teams do not necessarily suffer a loss of group connectedness'. They showed that performance indeed dipped during the pandemic if they did not replace their serendipitous old bonding of a walk down the hallway after a meeting with something equally effective. However, companies that implemented digital and hybrid-native practices to build and sustain bonding—like Dropbox and Mindbloom (winners of the 2022 Tony Hsieh Award for radical innovation in human capital)—saw their figures on strength of relationships go up into the range of 4.4 on a five-point scale.[8]

Further, I am not sure if cultures were truly built and sustained in offices, as we mostly believed. In the past several decades, all over the world, millions of dollars have been spent in culture building programmes, with consultants and trainers offering competing models to build cultures. However, there has been an equal amount of regret and lament that many companies have not been able to build a distinct culture. Are we, therefore, romanticizing the past and making ourselves believe that cultures got built because we were together in person? Or are we are making some attribution errors here—confusing physical buildings, heroic leaders and the culture rhetoric with true culture building? In any case, if culture is all about shared values, norms and behaviours, then why would the new world not throw up its own version of culture? If watching a CEO talk and lead a meeting in the physical world in an intimidating conference room was supposed to nurse the culture of a company, then why would her behaviour on a Zoom call not do the same?

Like in many other areas, in the working world too, new work models are challenging long-held beliefs about what culture is and how it gets built. The virtual, hybrid and gig-work models will redefine culture and present to us new horizons in this age-old area. Luckily, culture is not static. It is a social construct that changes with time. The new society, turbo-charged by virtual and collaborative technologies, will create culture 2.0 in this world.

To sum up

All these concerns originate from decades of habit, entrenched beliefs and the sheer inability to cope with the unfamiliar emerging future. The language of the past is not good enough to grasp and articulate the emergent reality of the future. With the pandemic and the rapid advancement of virtual, asynchronous work, we are compelled to find a new language to describe the emergent world of work. The search for feasibility is a trap. In other words, if we always asked whether it is feasible to go to the moon or climb the Everest, we would not have gone there. It took a leap of faith and commitment to undertake what must have then looked like an impossible adventure. We are at a similar inflection point regarding the course of work, both in India and globally. We could wait indefinitely for things to fall into place in some familiar ways. Or simply leap into the future and co-create a new world of work more suitable for the next generation.

12

Unleashing Human Capital

The Case for a National Ecosystem

*In the long history of humankind (and animal kind, too)
those who learned to collaborate and improvise most
effectively have prevailed.*

—Charles Darwin[1]

By now you may have been persuaded that the course of
the history of work is changing. You can see that flexible
work options are the way to go. But you would ask: how
do we get there? Can I, as an individual or as a firm, do
anything to advance this agenda? How will this address
the bigger question of human capital inclusion and support
the cause of taking urban jobs to India's burgeoning small
towns? Here are my thoughts on how to shape the *future
of work* and make it work for us, in India.

Let's think for a moment about ecosystems.
The *National Geographic* explains this very well:

An ecosystem is a geographic area where plants, animals, and other organisms, as well as weather and landscape, work together to form a bubble of life.[2] Every factor in an ecosystem depends on every other factor, either directly or indirectly. Unless we build and preserve robust ecosystems, many species on earth will not survive for long.

The same applies to this new species: flexible work options. They cannot exist in a vacuum. We must build a comprehensive ecosystem to enable, support and nurture the sustainable use of flexible work options as we embrace this dimension of the *future of work*. At a high level, we can think of five major actors that have to come together to build this ecosystem: i) government/policymakers, ii) industry bodies, (e.g. the Confederation of Indian Industry, National Association of Software and Services Companies [Nasscom]), iii) firms, iv) managers, and v) employees. If all these forces come together in cohesive and mutually complementary ways, we can not only deploy flexible work options at scale but also leverage them to deliver the intended goals. Again, consistent with the overall approach of this book, we will avoid manuals and cookie-cutter solutions. Let's look at what each of these actors can broadly do (in addition to, or to even reinforce, what they are already doing) to enable large-scale adoption of flexible work options.

What can India's Union and state governments do?

As discussed in the introduction to this book, we looked at building the ecosystem for remote work and other flexible work options closely through serious desk and field research during the pandemic. Let me first acknowledge the contributions of sixty-plus bright MBA students of the class of 2021 at the Indian School of Business and a few of my colleagues in contributing to the ideas outlined below. We identified five key factors that governments and policymakers must push for to create a favourable climate for remote work: i) hardware and broadband infrastructure, ii) Software and information security, iii) a policy framework for remote work and other forms of flexible working, iv) digital literacy and remote work-skills development for all citizens, and v) decongestion of urban areas and taking urban benefits to the small towns and villages.

A lot is happening in these areas. But lack of coordination and inability to adopt an integrated strategy is diluting the impact. Further, multiple ministries and government agencies handling various parts of these ecosystem factors are leading to duplication of effort, overlaps and lack of focus.

One possible solution is to create a 'national programme for *the future of work*' and bring in all related initiatives under one policy umbrella. Besides potentially breaking silos, it will signal the nation's commitment to be future-ready. Germany's government-sponsored *future of work* campaign, or the UK's efforts at placing a high-level official to steer *future of work* initiatives, are small beginnings in this direction. Governments all over the world are realizing the urgent need to anticipate and prepare their citizens for the *future of work*. India must take the lead and not wait to follow them. Besides finding a way to integrate many disparate programmes into an ecosystem, here are a few areas that need priority and futuristic attention in policymaking.

Hardware, work devices and broadband network

Ensuring large-scale access to affordable hardware, such as secure laptops and other work devices, and providing universal access to reliable, always-on high-speed broadband connectivity are fundamental to successful remote work.

Affordable and rugged laptops

Can governments at the Centre and in the states bring about helpful policies that make access to work devices affordable for all sections of society? Can the average cost of a durable laptop be brought down to Rs 10,000? These laptops do not require large storage space or application software, often added as a bundle to increase the value and price of a machine. It is only when everyone can afford a useful work device that there can be a level playing field in the matter of remote work for all types of workers—rich or poor, rural or urban (companies like Reliance Jio are moving in this direction).

It's time India took a bold step and encouraged mass-scale indigenous production of affordable, rugged video-enabled laptops or work devices that every working-age Indian can afford.

State of ICT infrastructure

For large-scale deployment of remote work, we not only need affordable devices but also next-generation ICT infrastructure that enables multimedia and immersive experiences at work, communication, collaboration and learning. Given the rapid technological changes, it will not be prudent to list the exact details. But the goal must be to leapfrog—as we have done in mobile telephony—and come up with next-gen data centres, server farms, cloud architecture, virtual desktop instances (VDI), data confidentiality and redundancy infrastructure, VPN servers and protocols for access measures. All these need to be expanded to accommodate the massive increase in encrypted traffic flows upon adoption of large-scale remote work.

Some of our recent investments in building our own semiconductors are in the right direction. But India has to find a way to make a step change in producing IT hardware and networking infrastructure to serve millions of its aspiring youth and seamlessly connect them to immersive, real-time, zero-latency networks and devices for work, learning and leisure.

Universal access to broadband Internet

In this context, it is important to take note of programmes like BharatNet. This programme is being implemented by Bharat Broadband Network Limited (BBNL), a central public sector undertaking, set up by the Department of Telecommunications, a department under Ministry of Communications of the Government of India for the establishment, management and operation of the National Optical Fibre Network to provide a minimum of 100 Mbit/s broadband connectivity to all 2,50,000-gram panchayats in the country, covering nearly 6,25,000 villages. Such programmes must be prioritized and executed with speed, with the same zeal as we are building our national highways. This can happen only if we start viewing the right to broadband Internet access as a 'fundamental right'. Though much smaller than India, many countries have started in this direction. Either through a legislative decision or judicial guidance, countries such as Costa Rica, Estonia, Finland, France, Greece and Spain are already moving in this direction. In India too, the Kerala High Court in 2019 held that the right to have access to the Internet is part of the fundamental right to education.[3]

Pushing our aspirations further, we can eventually aim at access to universal broadband Internet as a fundamental right for all citizens. India could lead this effort and be an example to the rest of the world. We have drawing room conversations around how, after *roti, kapda* and *makan*, it's the Internet. It's time those wishful conversations are made real.

Software and data security

We need an exclusive focus on developing extensive software that can run platforms to host and support remote work. Collaboration and video-conferencing tools must be advanced and made available up to the last mile. These will be viewed as firm-level efforts to be made, which is true. But a government that wants to promote remote and other forms of gig work must proactively track and encourage deployment of remote work-friendly software.

Cyber security and data privacy

We have a cyber-security policy with a set of lofty objectives. Similarly, we have just adopted the Digital Personal Data Protection Act 2023. This is a very positive and progressive move. However, lobbies and counter-lobbies—each representing its own vested interests— will continue to push back, and worse still, dodge true implementation of these regulations. It's ironic that the very same employers who want liberal regimes for data protection to gain access to more customers also push for stringent data protection when it comes to their employees. Such self-serving mindsets must be reminded constantly of the old saying: 'Eternal vigilance is the price of liberty'.

A national policy for remote work

Many countries and states within countries have started encouraging remote work through specific policy measures. Portugal introduced a legal framework for remote work, with rights and obligations for both employers and employees. Spain, Germany, Finland, Estonia and Canada are the other countries that have national policy frameworks for supporting remote work, including the right to ask for remote work, tax incentives for home offices, etc. In the middle of the pandemic in 2020, the US state of Colorado passed a law requiring employers to provide remote workers with the same benefits and protections as in-office workers. Much before the pandemic, way back in 2017, Japan introduced policy measures to encourage remote work with a view to decongest its big cities and provide work-life balance to its people.

Globally, some smaller cities have done pioneering work in encouraging remote work by incentivizing big-city folk to return to settle in those cities. 'Tulsa Remote'[4] was one such foresighted programme launched by the mayor of the city of Tulsa (population: only 4,13,066) in the landlocked south central state of Oklahoma in the

United States. Under this program, the authorities pay $10,000 to big-city workers to settle in this small town. Soon other smaller states like Vermont, Arkansas, Kansas and Alabama followed suit in attracting people from big metros like New York and San Francisco

Imagine the municipal commissioners of, say, Champaran, Motihari, Jaisalmer, Bharuch, Tirunelveli, Kottayam, Mysuru, Mayurbhanj or Midnapore incentivizing people to move away from Delhi, Mumbai and Bengaluru to work from these towns or cities? The knock-on effects of such a move on those small towns and districts will be tremendous. Together with incentives for industries to move to 'backward' areas, we could have policies that encourage city folk to enjoy rural serenity while they work.

One of the adverse consequences of remote working has been the tendency to end up overworking and be expected to join calls and answer emails much beyond one's normal working hours. To address this, many countries have provided 'right to disconnect' policies. France was the first country in the world to introduce the right to disconnect—even before the pandemic. Many others, like Italy, Spain, Belgium and the Philippines, have similar policies.

Many will say it looks too early and a luxury for India to think of such policies. But to believe that we can build a great country by burning out our citizens can be short-sighted.

Another post-pandemic 'gift' that has resulted is the 'digital nomad visa'. Many countries like Estonia, Germany, the Czech Republic and Spain have introduced digital nomad visas to encourage workers from other countries to work in their nations.

India too can take advantage of such a plan and invite foreigners to come and work out of Goa, Khajuraho, Konark,

Tiruchirappalli and Gokarna, for example, and boost our tourism while making these towns remote work friendly.

Incidentally, based on Nasscom's suggestion, an inter-ministerial working group was set up by the ministry of electronics and IT to enable a long-term blended work model with enablement for WFH on a permanent basis for IT/ITes workers. Certain relaxations in the SEZ rules regarding working from home were made. But we need to take a more long-term and comprehensive view of this emergent opportunity.

Indians should have the right to work remotely. It's time policymakers thought of it as a game-changing work model which will have huge multiplier effects on our rural economy and considered serious policy measures to encourage remote work and employment models.

Digital literacy and remote work skills

India is getting ready to be the world's third-largest economy in a fast-digitalizing world. However, its ranking in digital literacy and skills is quite low.[5] What is worse, the rural areas are lagging behind the rest of India in digital skills. While 66 per cent of people use the Internet in urban areas only 31 per cent do so in the rural areas.[6] As we build the India of the future, it will be imperative to accelerate our digital skills and readiness. This is a critical success factor for our economic growth. True, our skills missions are battling on many fronts and addressing India's vast skills gap. However, since digital literacy and basic digital skills have now emerged as life skills, we must prioritize them over all else and launch a 'movement' (not merely another government programme) to rapidly get millions of Indians, especially in rural India, ready for the inevitable digital future.

Working remotely calls for special skills

Just getting the opportunity to work from home or a remote location is not enough. Our reflexes are not trained to work remotely. While we like the freedom to work from anywhere, we may not know how to make the best use of it. Especially in India, where there are several first-time workers, we cannot assume that all will take to remote work with ease.

While there has been a lot of research and talk about what managers and organizations should do to make remote work effective, what individual workers should do has been less researched. It seems to have been assumed that while managers need to be taught to manage remote work, workers will learn it on their own. True, remote-first organizations like GitLab and Automattic, or successful adopters of remote work like Dropbox, etc., have documented some good practices that make remote work seamless,[7] however the focus is still on managers and organizational processes and not on the employee community.

Remote work as a default mode of work is new to all. We must all learn it together. There are no major precedents in recent history for remote work on a large scale. But approximately two years of remote work and another year of hybrid work have left us several lessons to learn. Even today, we need to be often told, 'Hey! Unmute and speak,' while on a Zoom call. Full-time remote work or work from anywhere needs some special skills to be effective. Learning to work asynchronously, inclusively and observing the etiquette of video-based meetings will be essential.

We believe that if all working-age citizens are taught, trained and exposed to these skills and mindsets (let's say, a crash course in *virtual work skills*), it will not only make them ready for life and work in the future but also add to the ecosystem for preparing a virtual work-ready workforce.

It's a pity that there are no major skilling programmes to get people work-ready. Getting job-ready is different from being work-ready. The transition from college to the formal world of work needs specific training in the skills we discussed. These will prepare one for work in the long run, irrespective of the job one does. Jobs in turn need domain skills. There is a strong case for imparting 'future-work ready' skills to all pre-college and undergraduate students. (In India, they will be in the plus-2 and bachelor's programmes) through a formally designed curriculum. This is like physical fitness training for a police officer before they are taught how to investigate a crime. Getting future-work ready is foundational, and it's a pity that we have not given much thought to it.

Making our small towns ready for the future of work

The ecosystem for encouraging new work models will not be complete unless we address the issue of how to make our tier-3 and tier-4 towns/cities more attractive to live, learn and grow in. Most of our employment occurs here in the small towns. But most of them are broken jobs, disguised unemployment and with less than subsistence wages. If this has to change, we must up-skill and upgrade not just rural workers but also employers, both in our small towns and big cities. For the big-city employer, the opportunity is to move jobs to small towns by using flexible work options. For the small-town employer, the opportunity is to spot talent locally, invest in local talent development and deploy more professional employment practices (like the Zoho experiment we discussed earlier).

We have 253 towns in India with populations of between 1 lakh and 10 lakh.[8] Beyond the obvious Beijing and Shanghai, China has 145 big cities. We have a comparable forty to forty-five. We need to build another fifty—to be specific, the next fifty. All these towns/cities must have advanced urban amenities, like good schools, colleges, hospitals, road/rail and air connectivity, reliable Internet access, co-working spaces and skill development programmes. If this is done programmatically, with clear markers and milestones, we will achieve two related and interdependent outcomes:

i.   If our small towns are 'liveable', our big cities will be liveable too. Big-city folk will migrate to the small towns and small-town folk will not migrate to the big cities. And both these are desirable outcomes. Reverse migration from the big cities to small towns and prevention of migration to the big cities can be stopped if we took a more holistic and ecosystem view of this problem.

ii.   During the pandemic, when workers were allowed to work from home and left the big cities, traffic on big-city roads improved dramatically, carbon emissions plummeted and city dwellers just breathed better. On the other hand, small towns which people went back to saw growth, with city-salary earners spending on local schools, apartments, restaurants and leisure activities. Ruchir Sarma, the well-known author and thinker on the subject of break-out growth, was surprised to see *jet skiing* in the small farm town of Varuna, about

15 kilometres away from the tier-2 town of Mysuru in Karnataka.[9]

In this context, we expect that the Union government's 'Rurban' mission will be to target the next fifty tier-3 and tier-4 cities, show measurable results, and then expand it to other village clusters.

Apart from what governments and policymakers can do, the role of industry bodies like the CII and Nasscom are equally important. Forecasting industry trends over the next five years, these bodies can lobby and educate governments to invest in policy initiatives. Nasscom has often done that. It was due to Nasscom's initiative that more flexible policies were brought about in the special economic zone (SEZ) rules. Responding to industry needs, the government today allows hybrid work for employees of SEZs until the end 2024.[10] Other major bodies, like the CII, FICCI, Employer's Federation, etc., are attempting to deal with the *future of work* implications. However, most discussions at the apex level of these bodies are about regulations, tax, compliance and international relations. Changing work models, workforce characteristics and new-age workspaces often remain as nice-to-have topics for conferences rather than matters requiring urgent action plans to be made.

Individual firms and managers—the other significant players in the ecosystem—have made some progress. Leaders and managers of several large firms have debated various aspects of the new ways of working, post-pandemic, and for a change these discussions have been very consultative with the larger employee body. But most of the responses to the new work models have been reactionary, opportunistic and expedient. All over the world, most firms and their managers have been wavering when it comes to handling the redesign of work. This is, of course, natural since we are in the early days of a whole new historic shift towards working differently. We have discussed at length in Chapter 5 what can organizations and managers do to embrace the *future of work* and reset their mindsets, styles and processes to build next-gen organizations. When and if all these changes are realized substantially, if not wholly, we will have strengthened the ecosystem for flexible work options.

Flexible work options, especially remote work, are not just a response to the pandemic. The pandemic itself is an early warning to humanity to prepare for bigger disruptions, like climate change and associated disasters. We are already experiencing the horrible consequences of global warming. Imagine how often people can go to a place called the office if every other day there are floods, earthquakes, fires and other calamities. India needs to get ready for far more turbulent times over the next decades. Staying prisoner of location, work model or outdated management habits will be in no one's interest. Let's use the twin gifts of the pandemic and digitalization and build a robust ecosystem that will make flexibility our new weapon to survive and to evolve the history of work towards a new course.

The *future of work* is largely about flexibility. We must learn to operationalize flexibility at three levels: i. Within ourselves as individuals; in our mindsets we must shed rigidly held beliefs from the past, ii. In organizations; they must be flexible about designing and offering new work models and leadership practices, and iii. At the state/ national levels, by creating policies that enable, encourage and create flexibility for all citizens, especially in matters of work and employment.

The Western narratives of the *future of work* provide us a great canvas to study and understand the subject. Instead of being enamoured or overwhelmed by this growing narrative, we must cherry-pick from their methods to adopt what suits India's vast human capital waiting to be unleashed through meaningful and well-paid jobs. Indiscriminate adoption of job-eliminating automation may not be in our best interest. On the other hand, remote work and other flexible work options that digital technologies offer can be used to our advantage, especially to empower human capital in small towns through decent wage-based formal employment.

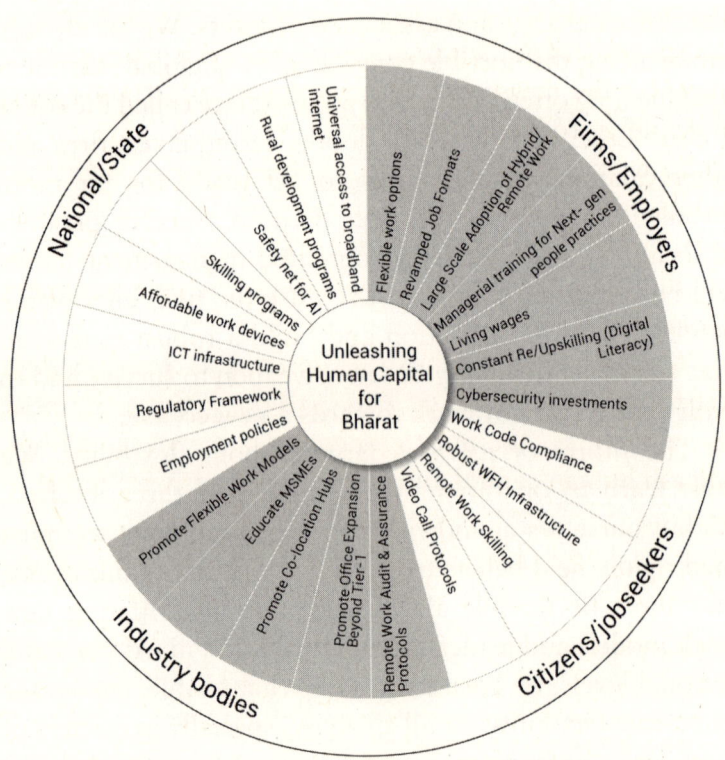

Ecosystem for unleashing human capital for Bharat

All this can happen only if there is a robust ecosystem for this, where employees, employers, managers, leaders, industry bodies, and state and union policies feed into each other and create the magic that ecosystems create.

The primary goal of this ecosystem must be to unleash the vast human capital of India. In turn, this needs building and adopting flexible work options. These options and new work models will need robust information and communication technologies across the country. Successful ICT will enable education, skills and employability. The next factor will be future-of-work-friendly regulations to enable flexible and inclusive work models, especially for rural India. As more of the next generation (Gen Z and Alpha) enter the workforce, they will demand higher flexibility. Employers will have to change and adapt their managerial and leadership styles to empower the new-generation employees and enable them to be more productive.

Now, it is easy to imagine that the gains of heightened productivity will, in turn, create new-age employment, leveraging ICT. Skills will feed into jobs and a decent living for all. Thus, a virtuous cycle will be set in motion, for Bharat and India

What our work for the future must be, is clear. We must fast-forward the *future of work* and not just watch it take its own course. We must embrace flexible work options, unleash human capital and converge Bharat with India.

Epilogue

*It is not a disaster to be unable to capture your ideal,
but it is a disaster to have no ideal to capture. It is not a
disgrace not to reach the stars, but it is a disgrace to have
no stars to reach for. Not failure, but low aim is sin.*

—Benjamin E. Mays[1]

15 August 2047—India's one-hundredth Independence Day. Bharat, that is India, is celebrating its advanced and seasoned nationhood. Counted now as citizens of a developed economy, Indians are rejoicing in their full-blown and wholesome freedom across many factors and scenarios:

I
Independence from the tyranny of organized work

Among other things, Indians have found an exciting, unique and world-leading aspect of independence: freedom from the tyranny of organized work. Over the last twenty years, Indian governments, employers and employees have steered a new movement of 'responsible autonomy and flexibility'. Employers now encourage employees to work form anywhere and agree on a few in-person meetings at mutually convenient locations and dates. The Union as well as state governments have offered a suite of progressive policies and incentives to encourage employers and employees to work from home and small towns. India Inc. has adopted and internalized all the developments in technology, and most of the repetitive, monotonous and non-rewarding work is now done by intelligent machines. Motivated by their new-found freedom around work time and space, Indians have imbibed a new code of responsible flexibility and autonomy. Overall, their health, well-being and productivity have gone up. Millions more Indians from small towns are now in well-paid jobs, thanks to the new flexible work models offered by all types of employers.

II
Home is for work, office for socializing

Seventy per cent of Indians across occupations, organizations and locations now have the flexibility to work from home or any place of their choice. Home is now the default location of work. If employers want employees to come to a place of work, it is explicitly and mutually agreed on as a condition of employment, which is honoured by both parties. Employees do want to come to central locations occasionally, to meet with colleagues and to share the joys of camaraderie. Most offices have moved nearer the home towns of people. Eight per cent of offices look very different from a few decades ago—no more the old-style cubicle farms of the 2020s. Offices now look more like lounges and hang-out zones for Gen Alpha.

Collaborative spaces allowing both small and large group interactions and sharing sessions have been built. There are large, immersive video walls, where those who can't join in person show up. Food, fun and frolic mark the new ethos of these occasional offices and neighbourhood co-location spaces. Flexible and green designs foster sustainability, making them attractive for the new generations. India leads the world trend in making home the new office and office the new club.

III
Every village has reliable broadband Internet

The Union government has recognized that access to reliable broadband Internet is a fundamental right of Indian citizens. Investing appropriate funds, Union and state governments have helped India leapfrog in providing uninterrupted access to the Internet. Internet penetration, which was about 50 per cent 2024, is now, in 2047, 90 per cent. Indians have complete access to the Internet despite the growth of their population. Public–private partnership and focused digital literacy programmes have prepared Indians to fully leverage the Internet for work, education, leisure and other economic activities. Learning from the experiences of smaller countries like Estonia, Greece and Finland—who by the mid-2020s had already provided universal broadband access to their citizens—the Indian government pursued a leapfrog strategy and provided Internet to all its villages. Such universal access to the Internet has transformed the labour market, allowing reliable access to remote work for people in the tiniest of villages. New-age global institutions (successors to the United Nations and World Bank—which were recreated to reflect the new power structure of the world in the 2030s) now attribute India's success in creating large-scale inclusive employment to its universalization-of-Internet strategy.

IV
India builds 500 more developed cities, towns , 'Rurban' clusters—engineering a reverse migration enabled by remote work

In the 2020s, India took note of the serious consequences of excessive migration of people from its rural towns to the big cities. As a result, the country accelerated its rural urbanization strategy and created several corridors, like the Delhi–Mumbai industrial corridor. One of its most successful programmes has been the Rurban mission. Under this, urban facilities such as roads, hospitals, schools, water, sanitation, trade development, skilling and training, etc., are provided to hundreds of village clusters. Earlier small towns, like Dibrugarh, Kharagpur, Sambalpur, Rajahmundry, Warangal, Hubbali, Dhanbad, Muzaffarnagar, Jaunpur and Kottayam have now become big places and are competing with Pune, Kochi and Jaipur. By 2047, a whole new set of Rurban clusters have come up, fully equipped to carry out all economic activities. Sample these village clusters across the country: Garividi (Andhra Pradesh), Tuting (Arunachal Pradesh), Hajo (Assam), Bettiah (Bihar), Madpal (Chhattisgarh), Rumla (Gujarat), Singla (Haryana), Hinner (Himachal), Behrabank (J&K), Birhu (Jharkhand), Tanalur-Nirmaruthoor (Kerala), Deshawadi (Madhya Pradesh), Kada (Maharashtra), Shangshak (Manipur), Sohkha (Meghalaya), Thingsulthliah (Mizoram), Kuarmunda (Odisha), Jalaal (Punjab), Namthang (Sikkim), Suthamalli (Tamil Nadu), Jukkal

(Telangana), Hrishyamukh (Tripura), Patehara (Uttar Pradesh), Dhanaulti (Uttarakhand) and Molian (West Bengal).[2]

In 2024, these areas were so nondescript that people living in these states did not know about their existence. However, now, in 2047, many across the states recognize them as vibrant centres of economic activity, fully capable of both localized and remote work-based employment.

Finally, Bharat and India have converged. Moving beyond the tier-1, tier-2 and tier-3 cities, India has embraced the tier-4, tier-5 and tier-6 towns, thus unravelling the vast potential of Bharat/India. Obviously, India is now able to develop and deploy future-ready human capital across the nooks and corners of its hinterland. Thirty per cent of the real estate (office space) in the erstwhile big cities of Mumbai, Gurugram, Bengaluru, etc., has been vacated, similar to what happened in New York and San Francisco in the mid-2020s. Much relieved, the residents of Bengaluru now take only about thirty minutes to commute to any place in the city, as opposed to two hours in the mid-2020s. Millions of jobs have moved to small towns, either physically or through remote/flexible work models.

V
India's SMEs are leading the world's flexibility index

Post the Covid-19 pandemic, in the mid-2020s, flexibility started gaining importance in the world of work. Since organized work across big and small firms continued to be stuck in the previous industrial-era regimentation, progressive firms, especially consulting firms wanting to build traction around flexibility, started tracking trends around it. One of the early indices was developed by

a little-known US company called Scoop, a carpooling
software company. But since commute time to workplaces
reduced significantly, post-pandemic, Scoop moved to
new areas and built a platform to enable hybrid work.
In the initial years, between 2022 and 2030, companies
all over the world were torn between what was practical,
convenient and futuristic and what were habitual, familiar
and legacy practices from the past. Quickly a mid-ground
was found: 'Hybrid work', a term no longer in use these
days, became the new norm for a period of time. Under this
arrangement, employers found a way to bring employees to
offices for at least two or three days of the week. However,
vast databases were being built to check what forms of
flexibility were being 'offered' by employers. Scoop built
an index around it. However, in the mid-2040s, employers
and employees settled down to flexibility as the natural
currency at work. Meanwhile, many indices were built to
measure and benchmark the move towards internalizing
flexibility across firm sizes. While the big firms over time
adopted flexibility, though reluctantly, the small firms with
less than 500 employees took the longest time to accept
the new normal. India's small firms were so entrenched
in 'presenteeism' that it was an agonizing transformation
for them to understand flexibility as both a business and
employee value proposition. Moving rapidly between
2035 and 2040, small and medium-sized firms, the
largest creators of regional employment in India, started
reimagining their work models and started to internalize
flexibility wholly and in the true spirit of the term. By
2047, to the surprise of the world (as it had been earlier
too, in the mid-2020s, at India's massive adoption of
technology, the miraculous growth of mobile phone usage
and payment gateways), most leading surveys and indices

in the world found Indian SMEs at the top of the flexibility charts. Once again India had leapfrogged, avoiding the tortuous course of the history of work taken by what were once called the advanced nations.

2047 and beyond, India emerges as the world's capital for human capital. Unleashed, India's human capital continues the journey to discover and shape the next new *future of work*.

Acknowledgements

It takes a village to write a book. This book is a result of nudging by many friends, colleagues, acquaintances, relatives and family members. They are so many that it is not practical to call out each of them.

ISB professors Madan Pillutla, S. Ramnarayan and Ram Nidumolu directly and indirectly nudged me, helped me clarify my thoughts and encouraged me.

Prof. Charles Dhanraj of Georgia State University, Atlanta, US, a long-time friend and well-wisher, helped me discover my potential for writing.

Prof. Amit Chauradia, Doane University, US, and Glory George, research associate, ISB, worked with me on the remote work research project during the pandemic, which helped me conceptualize the book and provided great insights.

Prof. T.V. Rao, former professor at IIM Ahmedabad and HRD guru, brought my efforts to fruition by connecting me to the editor of this book.

Thomas J. Menachery, research manager at ISB, gave me outstanding support and assistance in researching, proofreading, bouncing off ideas and handholding me through the process of writing.

Working with Prof. Ravi Gajendran, Florida International University, Miami, US, and Kalyan Kuppachi, ISB executive fellow programme in management (EFPM) scholar, on the research dissertation on the impact of hybrid work, refined my understanding with data and insights that have informed this book.

D.N.V. Kumara Guru, ISB, was immensely helpful in getting my book reviewed in advance by several thought leaders and getting their comments.

Rinku Paul, author and content specialist, patiently helped me with the initial research and drafting.

Radhika Marwah, the ever-helpful editor at Penguin Random House India, supported me immensely through this book project. Manali Das at Penguin helped with her diligent copy-editing.

Suresh Dutt Tripathi, formerly with Air India; B.P. Biddappa, HUL; and Zubin Palia, Tata Steel, shared their experiences and thoughts that enriched the book.

Vinay Agrawal, Tech Mahindra, helped me gain insights from many remote employees.

I thank Alok Ohrie, Amitabh Kant, Ashwin Yardi, Jayesh Ranjan, Lynda Gratton, Madan Pillutla, Pankaj Bansal, Prem Singh, Prithwiraj Choudhury, R.S. Pawar, Rajesh Nambiar, Ravi Gajendran, Rishikesha T. Krishnan, Rohit Kapoor and T.V. Rao for their advance review and generous comments.

My wife, Lakshmi, constantly boosted my morale, infused confidence, and gave me rock-solid emotional support and encouragement through the highs and lows of writing.

My loving daughters, Raagaleena and Spandana, and their respective spouses, Arun and Aditya, often urged me to write and contributed to enhancing my understanding of the next generation's aspirations through their personal experiences and insights.

Notes

Introduction

1 Ernst F. Schumacher, *Small Is Beautiful: Economics as if People Mattered*, London: Blond & Briggs, 1973.

2 'Pradhan Mantri Jan Dhan Yojana (PMJDY): National Mission for Financial Inclusion, Completes Nine Years of Successful Implementation', pib.gov.in, 28 August 2023, https://www.pib.gov.in/PressReleasePage.aspx?PRID=1952793.

3 'Total Direct Benefit Transfer (Cumulative)', Dbtbharat.gov.in, 15 April 2024, https://dbtbharat.gov.in.

4 'Statistics as of July 2023', Npci.org.in, 20 July 2023, https://www.npci.org.in/.

5 EY India, 'Reaping the Demographic Dividend', EY.Com, 11 April 2023, https://www.ey.com/en_in/india-at-100/reaping-the-demographic-dividend.

6 Ashish Kumar and Rishi Jain, 'India's Labour Scene Is Changing', *The Hindu BusinessLine*, 3 November 2023, https://www.thehindubusinessline.com/opinion/indias-labour-scene-is-changing/article67494591.ece#:~:text=The%20labour%20force%20participation%20rate,an%20increase%20in%20unemployed%20people.

7   McKinsey Global Institute, 'India's Turning Point: An Economic Agenda to Spur Growth and Jobs', www. mckinsey.com, 2020, https://www.mckinsey.com/featured-insights/india/indias-turning-point-an-economic-agenda-to-spur-growth-and-jobs.

8   Randstad, *Workmonitor 2022*, https://www.randstad.in/hr-news/workforce-insights/randstad-workmonitor/.

9   'The Long Walk of India's Migrant Workers in Covid-Hit 2020', *Indian Express*, 25 December 2020, https://indianexpress.com/article/india/the-long-walk-of-indias-migrant-workers-in-covid-hit-2020-7118809.
    'Over 1 Crore Migrant Labourers Return to Home States on Foot during Mar-Jun: Govt', *The Hindu*, 23 September 2020, https://www.thehindu.com/news/national/over-1-crore-migrant-labourers-return-to-home-states-on-foot-during-mar-jun-govt/article61702000.ece

10 Lukas Schlogl, Elias Weiss and Barbara Prainsack, 'Constructing the "Future of Work": An analysis of the policy discourse', *New Technology, Work and Employment*, 36, no. 3, 2021, pp. 307–26.

11 'Economic Survey 2022–23', Ministry of Finance, Government of India, 2023.

12 Arushi Kotecha, 'Ludhiana, Surat Now among Top 10 Cities Buying Luxury Cars', *Mint*, 26 July 2018, https://www.livemint.com/Industry/bo42kmJCtW2WDi6l2yj4yN/Ludhiana-Surat-now-among-top-10-cities-buying-luxury-cars.html

13 'The Future of Jobs Employment, Skills and Workforce Strategy for the Fourth Industrial Revolution', World Economic Forum, 2016.

Chapter 1

1   James Suzman, *Work: A History of How We Spend Our Time,* Bloomsbury Publishing, 2020.

2   David Foster Wallace, *This is Water: Some thoughts, Delivered on a Significant Occasion, about Living a Compassionate Life,* Hachette UK, 2009.

3   'Origins of Agriculture: the Nile Valley', *Encyclopedia Britannica,* 2019, https://www.britannica.com/topic/agriculture/The-Nile-valley.

4   Michael Kimmel, *Manhood in America,* Oxford University Press, New York, 2017.

5   Nikil Saval, *Cubed: The Secret History of the Workplace,* Anchor, 2015.

6   'The Decline of Privacy in Open-Plan Offices', BBC News, 30 July 2013, https://www.bbc.com/news/magazine-23502251.

7   S. Dixon, 'Social media use during COVID-19 worldwide: statistics & facts', Statista, 2022, https://www.statista.com/topics/7863/social-media-use-during-coronavirus-covid-19-worldwide

8   'U.S. Social Platform User Engagement Growth 2020', Statista, 2023, https://www.statista.com/statistics/265069/social-platform-user-engagement-change-usa/.
    'U.S. TikTok Users by Age 2020', Statista, 9 February 2023, https://www.statista.com/statistics/1095186/tiktok-us-users-age/.

9   Brooke Auxier, 'Activism on Social Media Varies by Race and Ethnicity, Age, Political Party', Pew Research Center, 2020, https://www.pewresearch.org/short-reads/2020/07/13/activism-on-social-media-varies-by-race-and-ethnicity-age-political-party.

Chapter 2

1   Attributed to Vladimir Lenin, the first and founding head of government of Soviet Russia from 1917 to 1924.

2   'Spring Festival Back to Work Day: 200 million people use DingTalk to work from home', China News,

2 March 2020, https://m.chinanews.com/wap/detail/zw/business/2020/02-03/9077412.shtml

3 'State of the American Workplace', Gallup, 2017, https://www.gallup.com/workplace/238085/state-american-workplace-report-2017.

4 'Hong Kongers Prefer Working in the Office', www.randstad.com.hk., 2018, https://www.randstad.com.hk/about-us/press-releases/working-at-the-office-a-popular-concept-among-hongkongers-randstad-workmonitor-research

5 Megan Tatum, 'Is the "Remote Work Window" about to Close?', BBC, 25 May 2022, https://www.bbc.com/worklife/article/20220519-is-the-remote-work-window-about-to-close.

6 Namrata Singh, 'Half of India Inc Bats for Full Office Return', *Times of India,* 21 November 2022, https://timesofindia.indiatimes.com/business/india-business/half-of-india-inc-bats-for-full-office-return/articleshow/95646212.cms

7 '71% Indian Jobseekers Choose Job Flexibility over High Salary: Indeed Survey', *India Today,* 18 August 2023, https://www.indiatoday.in/education-today/latest-studies/story/71-indian-jobseekers-choose-job-flexibility-over-high-salary-indeed-survey-2423188-2023-08-18

8 Ratna Bhushan and Prachi Verma, 'Hybrid Working Makes a Place for Itself at India Inc.', *Economic Times,* 15 September 2023, https://economictimes.indiatimes.com/jobs/hr-policies-trends/hybrid-working-makes-a-place-for-itself-at-india-inc/articleshow/103672376.cms

9 Jack Nilles, 'The telecommunications-transport tradeoff. Options for tomorrow and today', *California: Jala International,* 1973.

10 Nicholas Bloom, James Liang, John Roberts and Zhichun Jenny Ying, 'Does Working from Home Work? Evidence from a Chinese Experiment', *The Quarterly Journal of Economics,* vol. 130, issue 1, February 2015, pp. 165–218.

11 Prithwiraj Choudhury, Cirrus Foroughi and Barbara Larson, 'Work-from-anywhere: The productivity effects of geographic flexibility', *Strategic Management Journal* 42, no. 4, 2021, pp. 655–683.

12 Prithwiraj Choudhury, Tarun Khanna, Christos A. Makridis and Kyle Schirmann, 'Is Hybrid Work the Best of Both Worlds? Evidence from a Field Experiment', Harvard Business School Working Paper, no. 22-063, March 2022.

13 Gwynn Guilford, 'Need to Hire Workers in a Hot Job Market? Let Them Do Some Remote Work', *Wall Street Journal*, 5 August 2023, https://www.wsj.com/articles/need-to-hire-workers-in-a-hot-job-market-let-them-do-some-remote-work-506f72e6.

14 Kalyan Kuppachi, 'The impact of hybrid work arrangements on employee engagement and performance', Unpublished Dissertation (ISB EFPM programme). Supervised by Professors Chandrasekhar Sripada, Ravi Gajendran and S. Ramnarayan, 2023.

15 Annabelle Timsit, 'A Four-Day Workweek Pilot Was so Successful Most Firms Say They Won't Go Back', *Washington Post*, 21 February 2023, https://www.washingtonpost.com/wellness/2023/02/21/four-day-work-week-results-uk/.

Chapter 3

1 Robert C. Allen, 'Lessons from history for the future of work', *Nature*, 550, no. 7676, 2017, pp. 321–324.

2 John Maynard Keynes, 'Economic possibilities for our grandchildren', in *Essays in Persuasion*, London: Palgrave Macmillan UK, 1930, pp. 321–332.

3 'World-Renowned "Futurist" Looks 25 Years Ahead', ABC News, 2006, https://abcnews.go.com/GMA/Technology/story?id=2611827

4 Evan Andrews, 'Who Were the Luddites?' *HISTORY*, 26 June 2019, https://www.history.com/news/who-were-the-luddites.

5   'The Future of Jobs Report 2020', World Economic Forum, 2020.

6   Robert C. Allen, 'Lessons from history for the future of work', Nature, 550, no. 7676, 2017, pp. 321–324.

7   Joey George, 'Another essay about the future of work', *Journal of Information Technology Case and Application Research* 24, no. 1, 2022, pp. 3–11.

8   Prithwiraj Choudhury, Tarun Khanna, Christos A. Makridis and Kyle Schirmann, 'Is Hybrid Work the Best of Both Worlds? Evidence from a Field Experiment', Harvard Business School Working Paper, no. 22-063, March 2022.

9   Lynda Gratton, *Redesigning Work: How to Transform Your Organization and Make Hybrid Work for Everyone,* MIT Press, 2022.

10 H. Ford, 'Why do I favor five days' work with six days' pay?', interview with S. Crowther, World's Work, 1926, pp. 613–16.

11 'Principles for Responsible AI', NITI Aayog, 2021.

12 'GINI Index', World Bank, 2021, https://data.worldbank.org/indicator/SI.POV.GINI.

13 '"American Dream" Quickly Becoming an "Illusion"', says UN Human Rights Expert, UN News, 15 December 2017. News.un.org, https://news.un.org/en/story/2017/12/639652-american-dream-quickly-becoming-illusion-says-un-human-rights-expert

14 Lukas Schlogl, Elias Weiss and Barbara Prainsack, 'Constructing the "Future of Work": An Analysis of the Policy Discourse', *New Technology, Work and Employment* 36, no. 3, 2021, pp. 307–26.

15 Alice H. Amsden, *Escape from Empire: The Developing World's Journey through Heaven and Hell,* The MIT Press, 2007.

16 Deen Dayal Upadhyaya Grameen Kaushalya Yojana, https://www.india.gov.in/spotlight/deen-dayal-upadhyaya-grameen-kaushalya-yojana

Notes   169

17   Pradhan Mantri Gramin Digital Saksharta Abhiyan, https://
     www.pmgdisha.in/about-pmgdisha/

18   Bhaskar Chakravorti and Gaurav Dalmia, 'Is India the
     World's next Great Economic Power?', *Harvard Business
     Review*, 6 September 2023, https://hbr.org/2023/09/is-
     india-the-worlds-next-great-economic-power.

19   'What India's Workforce Thinks about Work Today',
     PricewaterhouseCoopers, 2022, https://www.pwc.in/what-
     indias-workforce-think-about-work-today.html.

Chapter 4

1   Sam Altman, 'Review of the Strength of Being
     Misunderstood', 2 December 2020, https://blog.samaltman.
     com/the-strength-of-being-misunderstood. (This quote is a
     slight alteration of what Sam said in his blog. By the way,
     Sam is against 'work from home'!)

2   'The Business Case for Flexible Working | CJ Talent
     Recruitment', CJ Talent, 2023, https://cjtalent.com/
     about-us-flexible-working-specialist-recruitment/flexible-
     working/.
     Zhao, Bhushan Sethi, Peter Brown and Yalin, 'Younger
     Workers Want Training, Flexibility, and Transparency',
     Strategy+Business, 31 October 2022, https://www.strategy-
     business.com/article/Younger-workers-want-training-
     flexibility-and-transparency.

3   Hickman & Robison (2020) Is Working Remotely
     Effective? Gallup Research Says Yes, https://www.gallup.
     com/workplace/283985/working-remotely-effective-
     gallup-research-says-yes.aspx.

4   'The Fluid Workforce Revolution', Capgemini Research
     Institute, 2020.

5   Ibid.

6   Lynda Gratton, 'How to do hybrid right', *Harvard Business
     Review* 99, no. 3, 2021, pp. 66–74.

7   'Work Patterns in the Federal Sector', Official Portal of the UAE Government, 2023, https://u.ae/en/information-and-services/jobs/working-in-uae-government-sector/work-patterns-in-the-federal-sector.

8   Gary Hamel and Michele Zanini, 'Humanocracy: Creating Organizations as Amazing as the People inside them', *Harvard Business Press*, 2020.

9   B. Sebastian Reiche, 'Between Interdependence and Autonomy: Toward a Typology of Work Design Modes in the New World of Work', *Human Resource Management Journal* (2023).

10   'How Haier Is Shattering the Status Quo', McKinsey, 2021, https://www.mckinsey.com/capabilities/people-and-organizational-performance/our-insights/shattering-the-status-quo-a-conversation-with-haiers-zhang-ruimin.

11   Nanette Fondas, 'Millennials say they'll relocate for work-life flexibility', *Harvard Business Review*, https://hbr.org/2015/05/millennials-say-theyll-relocate-for-work-lifeflexibility (2015).

12   Boris B. Baltes, Thomas E. Briggs, Joseph W. Huff, Julie A. Wright, and George A. Neuman, 'Flexible and Compressed Workweek Schedules: A Meta-analysis of their Effects on Work-Related Criteria', *Journal of Applied Psychology* 84, no. 4, 1999, p. 496.

13   Nicole V. Shifrin and Jesse S. Michel, 'Flexible Work Arrangements and Employee Health: A Meta-Analytic Review', *Work & Stress* 36, no. 1, 2022, pp. 60–85.

14   Greta Onken-Menke, Stephan Nüesch and Claudia Kröll, 'Are you Attracted? Do you Remain? Meta-Analytic Evidence on Flexible Work Practices', *Business Research* 11, 2018), pp. 239–77.

15   Flex Index Report Q3, Scoop, 2024.https://www.flex.scoopforwork.com/stats?utm_source=press&utm_medium=article&utm_campaign=flex-report-q3

16 'The Flex Index: World's Largest Source of Hybrid, Remote Work Reqs', Scoop for Work, https://www.flex.scoopforwork.com/.

17 Dr Gleb Tsipursky, 'The Death of Full-Time In-Office Work and the Rise of Tomorrow's Corporate Titans', *Forbes*, 16 August 2023, https://www.forbes.com/sites/glebtsipursky/2023/08/16/the-death-of-full-time-in-office-work-and-the-rise-of-tomorrows-corporate-titans

Chapter 5

1 The quote is often associated with the Bible. Jesus, responding to the questions of his disciple Thomas, urges him to repose faith in God and believe. We have used this to signify that it will take us a leap of faith to use remote work options for non-IT workers. We will see it happen if we believe it can happen.

2 Susan Lund, Anu Madgavkar, James Manyika and Sven Smit, 'What's Next for Remote Work: An Analysis of 2,000 Tasks, 800 Jobs, and Nine Countries', McKinsey. www.mckinsey.com, 23 November 2020, https://www.mckinsey.com/featured-insights/future-of-work/whats-next-for-remote-work-an-analysis-of-2000-jobs-and-nine-countries.

3 Prithwiraj Choudhury and Susie L. Ma, 'Unilever: Remote Work in Manufacturing', Harvard Business Publishing Education case, oroduct #: 622030-PDF-ENG, 2022.

4 'The Future of Work in Manufacturing', Deloitte Insights, 2019, https://www2.deloitte.com/us/en/insights/industry/manufacturing/future-of-work-manufacturing-jobs-in-digital-era.html.

5 'COMMAND for Dozing | Cat | Caterpillar', 2023.

6 'Factory Innovation Post COVID-19', Gartner Research & Insights, 2022, https://www.gartner.com/en/supply-chain/trends/factory-innovation.

7   Mayank Agrawal, Karel Eloot, Matteo Mancini and
     Alpesh Patel, 'Industry 4.0: Reimagining Manufacturing
     Operations after COVID-19', McKinsey, 29 July 2020,
     https://www.mckinsey.com/capabilities/operations/
     our-insights/industry-40-reimagining-manufacturing-
     operations-after-covid-19.
8   '25 Million New Jobs in Indian Retail Sector by 2030:
     Study', *The Hindu*, 8 March 2021, https://www.
     thehindu.com/business/Industry/25-million-new-jobs-
     in-indian-retail-sector-by-2030-study/article34020291.
     ece#:~:text=Around%2025%20million%20new%20
     jobs,%2C%20job%20creation%2C%20and%
     20exports.

Chapter 6

1   Attributed to a 1963 speech by US President John F. Kennedy.
     The quote was also in usage earlier.
2   Valerie Cerra, 'An Inclusive Growth Framework', in
     How to Achieve Inclusive Growth, edited by Valerie
     Cerra, Barry Eichengreen, Asmaa El-Ganainy and Martin
     Schindler, Oxford University Press, 2022.
3   *Gurujadalu*, complete works of Gurajada, editors: Sri
     Pennepalli Gopalakrishna, Dr Kalidasu Purushotham and
     Sri Mannem Rayudu, MANASU Foundation, Hyderabad,
     first edition, 21 September 2012.
4   Gary S. Becker, *Human Capital: A Theoretical and
     Empirical Analysis, with Special Reference to Education*,
     University of Chicago Press, 2009.
5   'Opportunities for All: A Framework for Policy Action on
     Inclusive Growth', OECD, 2018.
6   Ibid.
7   Rafael Ranieri and Raquel Almeida Ramos, 'Inclusive
     growth: Building up a concept', no. 104, working paper,
     International Policy Centre for Inclusive Growth (IPC-IG),
     2013.

8   Simon Kuznets, 'Economic Growth and Economic Inequality', *American Economic Review* 45, 1955, pp. 1–28.

9   Amartya Sen, *Development as Freedom*, Oxford University Press, 1999.

10   'Economic Survey 2022–23', Ministry of Finance, Government of India, 2023.

11   'Dropout Rates in Schools in India', Education for All in India, 13 April 2023, https://educationforallinindia.com/dropout-rates-in-schools-in-india.

12   'Annual Status of Education Report', 2022, Aser, https://Asercentre.org/. https://asercentre.org/aser-2022/.

13   'Talent Shortage: What Workers Want', Manpower Group, 2023, https://www.manpowergroup.co.in/talent-shortage.html

14   '80% of Indian Engineers Not Fit for Jobs, Says Survey', *Business Today*, 25 March 2019, https://www.businesstoday.in/latest/corporate/story/indian-engineers-tech-jobs-survey-80-per-cent-of-indian-engineers-not-fit-for-jobs-says-survey-181442-2019-03-25

15   Wheebox India Skills Report 2023, Wheebox, 2023.

16   New Education Policy (2020), Policy document released by Government of India, https://www.education.gov.in/sites/upload_files/mhrd/files/NEP_Final_English.pdf

17   'Fewer Women Have Jobs as India's Population Soars', Al Jazeera, 10 April 2023, https://www.aljazeera.com/gallery/2023/4/10/as-indias-population-soars-number-of-women-in-workforce-shrinks

18   'The Power of Parity: Advancing Women's Equality in Asia Pacific', McKinsey & Company, 2018, https://www.mckinsey.com/featured-insights/gender-equality/the-power-of-parity-advancing-womens-equality-in-asia-pacific.

Chapter 7

1   PM Modi at the 36th Convocation ceremony of Gandhigram Rural Institute, 11 November 2022, https://

www.narendramodi.in/prime-minister-narendra-modi-attends-convocation-of-gandhigram-rural-institute-in-tamil-nadu-565766.

2   '"Bharat" Users at Par with "India" Users When it Comes to Participating in Online Financial Activities: Report', *The Hindu BusinessLine*, 29 January 2022, https://www.thehindubusinessline.com/info-tech/bharat-users-at-par-with-india-users-when-it-comes-to-participating-in-online-financial-activities-report/article64944849.ece#:~:text=In%20terms%20of%20choice%20of,wallets%20multiple%20times%20a%20week.

3   Romita Majumdar, '52% of Indian Population Had Internet Access in 2022, Says Report', *Economic Times*, 3 May 2023, https://economictimes.indiatimes.com/tech/technology/52-of-indian-population-had-internet-access-in-2022-says-report/articleshow/99964704.cms

4   Lata Jha, 'Bharat Goes Online in a Big Way, Says Google Report', *Mint*, 9 May 2019, https://www.livemint.com/technology/tech-news/bharat-goes-online-in-a-big-way-says-google-report-1557393668958.html.

5   Surabhi, 'India's "Middle Cities" to Overtake Metros in Driving Consumption', *The Hindu BusinessLine*, 18 March 2021, https://www.thehindubusinessline.com/data-stories/data-focus/indias-middle-cities-to-overtake-metros-in-driving-consumption/article34100583.ece#:~:text=On%20the%20other%20hand%2C%20'middle,rise%20of%20India's%20Middle%20Cities'.

6   'India to Have 17 out of 20 Fastest-Growing Cities Globally between 2019-2035: Report', Moneycontrol, 7 December 2018, https://www.moneycontrol.com/news/business/economy/india-to-have-17-out-of-20-fastest-growing-cities-globally-between-2019-2035-report.

7   Faizan Haidar, 'Tier-II Cities Emerging as Growth Frontier in Office and Retail Sector: Report', *Economic Times*, 20 October 2022, https://economictimes.indiatimes.com/

industry/services/property-/-cstruction/tier-ii-cities-emerging-
as-growth-frontier-in-office-and-retail-sector-report.

8 'Why Myntra's Sales Announce the Quiet Rise of Small-Town
India', *Live Mint*, 6 December 2022, https://www.livemint.
com/opinion/online-views/why-myntra-s-sales-announce-
the-quiet-rise-of-small-town-india-11670306278457.
html#:~:text=In%20a%20recent%20media%20
interaction,Tier%202%20cities%20and%20beyond.

9 Mohanbir Sawhney, '7 Ways Amazon Is Winning by Acting
"Glocally" in India', *Forbes*, 2018, https://www.forbes.com/
sites/mohanbirsawhney/2018/04/30/7-ways-that-amazon-
is-winning-by-acting-glocally-in-india/?sh=1dda83f661c1

10 'Walmart Focuses on Growing India's Unique Ecosystem',
Corporate.walmart.com, 2023, https://corporate.walmart.
com/news/2023/05/12/walmart-focuses-on-growing-
indias-unique-ecosystem

11 Sagar Malviya, 'Small Towns Outpace Cities in Demand
for Baby Care Items', *Economic Times*, 25 August 2022,
https://economictimes.indiatimes.com/industry/cons-
products/fmcg/small-towns-outpace-cities-in-demand-for-
baby-care-items/articleshow/93762193.cms.

12 'Nestle India on Path to Accelerated Growth in Rural Areas,
Prices of Some Commodities Still a Concern, Says CMD',
ETRetail, 17 February 2023, https://retail.economictimes.
indiatimes.com/news/food-entertainment/personal-care-
pet-supplies-liquor/nestle-india-on-path-to-accelerated-
growth-in-rural-areas-prices-of-some-commodities-still-a-
concern-says-cmd/97997949.

13 'Why Skill Based Courses are Catching up among Students
Going to Study Abroad', *Financial Express,* 14 April 2022,
https://indianexpress.com/article/education/study-abroad/
skill-based-courses-growing-popular-among-study-abroad-
aspirants-experts-explain-7907364/#:~:text=Apart%20
from%20the%20factor%20of,same%20course%-
20at%20foreign%20universities.

14   Bharat: The Neo India Report, Sharechat and GroupM, 2022.

15   'Why Myntra's Sales Announce the Quiet Rise of Small-Town India', Live Mint, 6 December 2022, https://www.livemint. com/opinion/online-views/why-myntra-s-sales-announce-the-quiet-rise-of-small-town-india-11670306278457. html#:~:text=In%20a%20recent%20media%20 interaction,Tier%202%20cities%20and%20beyond.

16   'Funding for Start-ups in Small Towns Surges 41%, Bengaluru, Mumbai, NCR See Decline: Blume Report', Moneycontrol, 6 March 2023, https://www.moneycontrol. com/news/business/startup/funding-for-startups-in-small-towns-surges-41-bengaluru-mumbai-ncr-see-decline-blume-report-10207491.html

17   Kala Vijayraghavan and Lijee Philip, 'Brands Now Rope in Regional Influencers to Win over Small Towns, Villages', *Economic Times*, 16 July 2022, https://economictimes. indiatimes.com/tech/technology/brands-now-rope-in-regional-influencers-to-win-over-small-towns-villages/ articleshow/92907338.cms

18   'Emerging Technology Hubs of India', NASSCOM and Deloitte, 2023.

19   'SPMRM | Ministry of Rural Development | GOI', Rurban. gov.in, https://rurban.gov.in/index.php/public_home/about_us

Chapter 8

1   Mahatma Gandhi, *Collected Works of Mahatma Gandhi*, 1967. The Collected Works of Mahatma Gandhi (Electronic Book), Publications Division Government of India, New Delhi, 1999, 98 volumes.

2   Michael Lipton, 'Urban bias and inequality', in Mitchell A Seligson (ed.), *The Gap Between Rich And Poor: Contending Perspectives On The Political Economy Of Development*, Routledge, 1985, pp. 89–94.

3   Raghuram Rajan and Rohit Lamba, *Breaking the Mould: Reimagining India's Economic Future*, Penguin Random House India, Gurugram, 2023.

4   Talent Trends Report 2022, Randstad, 2022.

5   Rahul Aripaka, 'Watch out India, Now Bharat has Started to Rise', *Economic Times*, 12 April 2023, https://economictimes.indiatimes.com/news/economy/indicators/watch-out-india-now-bharat-has-started-to-rise/articleshow/99436074.cms

6   Supriya Roy, 'Zoho India FY22 Profit Rises 43% to Rs 2,748.83 Crore', *Economic Times*, 29 January 2023, https://economictimes.indiatimes.com/tech/startups/zohos-profit-rises-43-to-over-rs-2700-crore-in-fy22/articleshow/97418716.cms.

7   'Zoho', 2023, https://www.zoho.com/.

8   'Croatia Digital Nomad Visa: The Ultimate Guide', Nomad Capitalist, 19 May 2023, https://nomadcapitalist.com/expat/croatia-digital-nomad-visa/.

9   'Japan Is Paying Families 1 Million Yen per Child to Move out of Tokyo', NDTV, 3 January 2023, https://www.ndtv.com/world-news/families-will-get-1-million-yen-to-leave-tokyo-heres-why-3661458.

Chapter 9

1   Attributed to the American architecture critic Ada Louise Huxtable (1921–2013).

2   'India's Population Expected to Rise till 2050 and Then Decline: UN', NDTV, 19 April 2023, https://www.ndtv.com/india-news/indias-population-expected-to-rise-till-2050-and-then-decline-un-3961880.

3   'Work Trend Index: Microsoft's Latest Research on the Ways we Work', www.microsoft.com, 22 September 2022, https://www.microsoft.com/en-us/worklab/work-trend-index/.

4   'US Workforce Confidence Index', Economicgraph. linkedIn.com, 2022, https://economicgraph.linkedin.com/ workforce-data/us-workforce-confidence-index.

5   'What Workforce Diversity Means for Gen Z'. Monster. com, 2023, https://hiring.monster.com/resources/workforce-management/diversity-in-the-workplace/workforce-diversity-for-millennials/.

6   'Generation Disconnected: Data on Gen Z in the Workplace', Gallup.com, 11 November 2022, https://www.gallup.com/ workplace/404693/generation-disconnected-data-gen-workplace.aspx.

7   'Welcome to Gen-Z', Deloitte, 2018.

8   Gen Z Research, Fiverr Press, 2023, https://www.fiverr. com/news/gen-z-research

9   Edward L. Deci, 'Effects of Externally Mediated Rewards on Intrinsic Motivation', *Journal of Personality and Social Psychology* 18, no. 1, 1971, p. 105.

10   Daniel H. Pink, *Drive: The Surprising Truth about what Motivates us,* Penguin, 2011.

11   'Millennials: Burden, Blessing, or Both?', McKinsey, 2016, www.mckinsey.com. https://www.mckinsey.com/ capabilities/people-and-organizational-performance/our-insights/millennials-burden-blessing-or-both.

Chapter 10

1   Attributed to the German physicist Georg Christoph Lichtenberg (1742–99).

2   Milton Friedman, 'The Social Responsibility of Business is to Increase Its Profits', *New York Times*, 13 September 1970, https://www.nytimes.com/1970/09/13/archives/a-friedman-doctrine-the-social-responsibility-of-business-is-to.html.

3   R.A.G. Monks and N. Minow, 'Corporate Governance on Equity Ownership and Corporate Value', *Journal of Financial Economics* 20, no. 3, 1995, pp. 293–315.

Catherine M. Daily, Dan R. Dalton and Albert A. Cannella Jr, 'Corporate Governance: Decades of Dialogue and Data', *Academy of Management Review* 28, no. 3, 2003, pp. 371–382.

Ruth V. Aguilera, Igor Filatotchev, Howard Gospel and Gregory Jackson, 'An Organizational Approach to Comparative Corporate Governance: Costs, Contingencies, and Complementarities', *Organization Science* 19, no. 3, 2008, pp. 475–92.

4   Uday Kotak, Report of the Committee on Corporate Governance, Securities and Exchange Board of India, 2017.

5   Tsedal Neeley, *Remote Work Revolution: Succeeding from Anywhere, Harper Business*, New York, 2021.

6   Paul Krugman, 'Wonking Out: Is the Great Resignation a Great Rethink?', *New York Times*, 5 November 2021, sec. Opinion, https://www.nytimes.com/2021/11/05/opinion/great-resignation-quit-job.html.

7   Lynda Gratton and Andrew J. Scott, *The 100-Year Life: Living and Working in an Age of Longevity*, Bloomsbury Publishing, 2016.

8   Sahara Sadik and Phillip Brown, 'Corporate Recruitment Practices and the Hierarchy of Graduate Employability in India', *Oxford Review of Education* 46, no. 1, 2020, pp. 96–110.

9   TCS National Qualifier Test: Corporates, www.tcsion.com, https://www.tcsion.com/hub/national-qualifier-test-corporates/.

10   'Skills-First: Reimagining the Labor Market and Breaking Down Barriers', LinkedIn Economic Graph, 2023, https://economicgraph.linkedin.com/content/dam/me/economicgraph/en-us/PDF/skills-first-report-2023.pdf

11   Marcus Buckingham and Ashley Goodall, 'Reinventing Performance Management', *Harvard Business Review* 93, no. 4, 2015, pp. 40–50.

12   Jena McGregor, 'The Corporate Kabuki of Performance Reviews', *Washington Post*, 14 February 2013, https://www.washingtonpost.com/national/on-leadership/the-corporate-kabuki-of-performance-reviews/2013/02/14/59b60e86-7624-11e2-aa12-e6cf1d31106b_story.html.

13   Penelope Sue Greenberg, Ralph H. Greenberg and Yvonne Lederer Antonucci, 'Creating and Sustaining Trust in Virtual Teams', *Business Horizons* 50, no. 4, 2007, pp. 325–33.

14   'Survival of the Richest: The India Story', Oxfam India, 15 January 2023. www.oxfamindia.org, https://www.oxfamindia.org/knowledgehub/workingpaper/survival-richest-india-story#:~:text=Oxfam%20India.

15   Derek Saul, 'CEOs Made 324 Times More than Their Median Workers in 2021, Union Report Finds', *Forbes*, 2022, https://www.forbes.com/sites/dereksaul/2022/07/18/ceos-made-324-times-more-than-their-median-workers-in-2021-union-report-finds/?sh=7db84326ac52.

16   Bhaswar Kumar, 'How Can We Solve India Inc's High CEO Pay Problem?' @Bsindia, *Business Standard*, 11 August 2022, https://www.business-standard.com/podcast/current-affairs/how-can-we-solve-india-inc-s-high-ceo-pay-problem-122081100078_1.html.

17   Burrhus Frederic Skinner, 'Superstition in the Pigeon', *Journal of Experimental Psychology* 38, no. 2, 1948, p. 168.

18   Alfie Kohn, 'Why Incentive Plans Cannot Work', *Harvard Business Review* 71, no. 5, 1993, p. 54.

19   Ganesh Janan, 'Stop Making Fun of Managers', *Financial Times*, 24 February 2023, https://www.ft.com/content/48fd4416-b4e1-444e-b89f-041deb7de200.

20   Jim Harter, 'U.S. Employee Engagement Needs a Rebound in 2023', Gallup.com, 25 January 2023, https://www.gallup.com/workplace/468233/employee-engagement-needs-rebound-2023.aspx.

21   '23% Employees in India Are Not Actively Engaged in the Workplace, Says a Survey – ETHRWorld', *Economic Times,* 29 June 2022, https://hr.economictimes.indiatimes.com/news/workplace-4-0/employee-engagement/23-employees-in-india-are-not-actively-engaged-in-the-workplace-says-a-survey/92549625.

22   Chandrasekhar Sripada 2022. Remote Work Survey in a leading pharma company, India, unpublished in-company survey report.

23   Penelope Sue Greenberg, Ralph H. Greenberg and Yvonne Lederer Antonucci, 'Creating and Sustaining Trust in Virtual Teams', *Business Horizons* 50, no. 4, 2007, pp. 325–333.

24   Prithwiraj Choudhury, Cirrus Foroughi and Barbara Larson, 'Work-from-anywhere: The productivity effects of geographic flexibility', *Strategic Management Journal* 42, no. 4, 2021, pp. 655–683.

25   Daniel H. Pink, *Drive: The Surprising Truth about What Motivates Us,* Penguin, 2011.

26   Dan Ariely, Uri Gneezy, George Loewenstein and Nina Mazar, 'Large stakes and big mistakes', *Review of Economic Studies* 76, no. 2, 2009, pp. 451–69.

Chapter 11

1   Kenneth Burke, *Permanence and Change: An Anatomy of Purpose*, University of California Press, 1935.

2   Internet Adoption in India, IAMAI and Nielsen, 2021.

3   Ibid.

4   'Wipro Fires 300 Employees for Moonlighting', *The Hindu*, 21 September 2022, sec. Industry, https://www.thehindu.com/business/Industry/wipro-fires-300-employees-for-moonlighting/article65918759.ece.

5   Susan G. Cohen and Gerald E. Ledford Jr, 'The Effectiveness of Self-Managing Teams: A Quasi-Experiment', *Human Relations* 47, no. 1, 1994, pp. 13–43.

John P. Millikin, Peter W. Hom and Charles C. Manz, 'Self-Management Competencies in Self-Managing Teams: Their Impact on Multi-Team System Productivity', *Leadership Quarterly* 21, no. 5, 2010, pp. 687–702.

6   Rini van Solingen, *How to Lead Self-managing Teams?: A Business Novel on Changing Leadership from Sheepherding to Beekeeping*, Createspace Independent Pub., 2016.

7   Lars Kolind and Jacob Bøtter, *Unboss*, Jyllands-Postens Forlag, Aarhus, 2012.

8   'Boost your collaboration to become a top remote and hybrid working team', World Economic Forum, 2023, https://www.weforum.org/agenda/2023/04/remote-hybrid-working-collaboration/.

Chapter 12

1   Attributed to Charles Darwin (1809–1882) English naturalist, geologist and biologist.

2   'Ecosystem | National Geographic Society', Education. nationalgeographic.org. *National Geographic*, 1 May 2023, https://education.nationalgeographic.org/resource/ecosystem/.

3   'Access to Internet Is a Basic Right, Says Kerala High Court', *The Hindu*, 19 September 2019, https://www.thehindu.com/sci-tech/technology/internet/access-to-internet-is-a-basic-right-says-kerala-high-court/article29462339.ece.

4   https://www.tulsaremote.com/

5   'India: Internet Literacy Index by Category 2021', Statista, 22 December 2022, https://www.statista.com/statistics/1232343/internet-literacy-index-by-category-india/#:~:text=In%202021%2C%20India%20had%20a%20rank%20of.

6   'India: Urban Rural Gaps in Digital Literacy by Internet Activity', Statista, 2020, https://www.statista.com/statistics/1389943/india-urban-rural-gaps-in-digital-

literacy-by-internet-activity/#:~:text=Urban%2Drural%20
gaps%20in%20digital.

7   'GitLab's Guide to All-Remote', *The GitLab Handbook*,
     2023,   https://handbook.gitlab.com/handbook/company/
     culture/all-remote/guide/.

8   'List of Cities in India by Population', Wikipedia, 7 December
     2023,   https://en.wikipedia.org/wiki/List_of_cities_in_
     India_by_population#cite_note-PaschimChamparan-24.

9   Ruchir Sharma, 'An Economic Miracle in India', *Financial
     Times*, 7 May 2023, https://www.ft.com/content/07a246d3-
     db87-4803-b900-f891c49686ad.

10   Nexdigm Private Limited, 'Government Allows "Hybrid
     Working" for SEZ Employees until December 2024",
     Mondaq,   14   November   2023,   https://www.mondaq.
     com/india/employee-rights-labour-relations/1388742/
     government-allows-hybrid-working-for-sez-employees-
     until-december-2024.

Epilogue

1   Attributed to Benjamin E. Mays (1894–1984), American
     rights leader.

2   These names were taken randomly from the government
     report at https://rurban.gov.in/index.php/Public_reports/
     approved_clusters#gsc.tab=0)

Beyond the Book

Call for Action

This book is aimed not only to stimulate ideas but also to encourage and support real-world changes and actions on the ground. There are *five* major goals of this book:

1. Help decongest big cities;
2. Develop semi-urban rural towns;
3. Provide greater level playing field and access to jobs for people in remote non-metro places;
4. Prevent avoidable 'migration' of small-town talent to big cities; and
5. Make India a great country for sustainable and enjoyable work.

To achieve these goals, some of the actions we all can take will include:

1. Embrace and adopt more flexibility at work and in organizations;
2. Leverage new-age technology to make work easy, accessible and productive for all;

3. Adopt remote and hybrid work formats with conviction and at scale;
4. Build and enhance the ecosystem that supports and promotes taking jobs to people (not people to jobs); and
5. Prioritize and focus on shaping a *future of work* conducive to India, creating more jobs and using automation more prudently.

Many more actions can be conceived, designed, experimented, executed, measured and documented. And I know that millions of citizens and like-minded readers can lend a hand to take the ideas of this book forward. We need many more ideas and actions to snowball this attempt into an organizational, social and national movement.

I invite all the readers, their friends, relatives and associates (in India and overseas) to join the following 'LinkedIn Group' (Shaping the Future of Work for India and Bharat) and share their ideas, seek and give help, and make this book a living document.

Please scan this QR code and join me and others on the LinkedIn group.

Scan QR code to access the
Penguin Random House India website